The All-Time Themed Baseball Teams
Copyright © 2016-2017 by Paul Steinman

All rights reserved. No part of this book may be reproduced or transmitted in any form or by any means without written permission from the author.

ISBN (978-0-9991288-0-0)

Printed in USA by Amazon

Dedication

This book is dedicated to my wife Elizabeth for putting up with my sports addiction, encouraging me to fulfill my goal to write a book and most of all for inspiring me throughout the writing process. Without her encouragement, understanding and occasional nudge to write, this book would not be a reality (So if you don't like it, blame my wife).

To my mom, you always encouraged me in all my pursuits and had more faith in me than I did myself. I miss you and wish you could be here to read it. I'm sure you are smiling somewhere and happy that there was never a Trump to play baseball.

To my three children, Sam, Audrey and Joe; thank you for allowing me some time to write. You have all shown some interest in baseball and more recently interest in some of the unique names associated with the game. I agree Nick Swisher should have been a basketball player and I appreciate your encouragement and I hope you will enjoy this book. Better yet, I hope you get all your friends to buy it. See if you can find yourselves on the book cover.

To Lisa, Mary and Dino Castellani, wife and children of my departed fraternity brother and friend Tony aka Keg. I will miss your husband/dad and will forever remember him jumping for joy (more hops than anyone realized) in celebration of the 1986 Mets' World Series victory. Tony's numerous inputs over the years contributed greatly to the book and the all body part team in particular. Sorry my old friend, I did not include Dick Pole on the all-time body-part team.

To the Dwyer family – Several years ago, when I showed you an initial draft of the book, you all showed such interest in the concept that it helped me to move forward writing it even when it was not the foremost thought on my mind. I have not forgotten that you said you would buy a copy if I ever finished it.

To Andrew Schmolka – My book editor. A true baseball fan, lawyer extraordinaire, and friend. You graciously agreed to my request to edit this book without anything in return. I appreciate the time you put into it, the constructive feedback, keen insight and above all, your friendship. Of course, all grammer and spealing errers are your fawlt ☺.

To the New Castle Nighthawks – It has been an honor coaching you guys and seeing you develop your baseball skills. I off course expect you to each buy several copies of this book and to keep turning dem hips while you turn dem pages.

Finally, the dedication would not be complete without recognizing two of my long-time friends -- Ivan Bergstein and Barry Bear. With all of our discussions over the years dating back to high school and college including those late night phone calls and more recently email and text messages, you guys set the foundation for the origins of this book and were the true inspirations for me to see it through to completion. If there was an all-time friend's team, the two of you would be on it with Barry batting second to sacrifice me over and Ivan of course batting clean-up looking for the homerun (but most likely striking out)☺. To the two of you, I will save you the trouble of asking and/or reading (but not buying) and tell you now that Sixto Lizcano and Josh Reddick are not going to be candidates for the all body-part team. Maybe there is a place for them in my next book.

Table of Contents

Preface 9

Introduction 13

The All-Time Themed Baseball Teams, Volume 1:

Chapter - Theme	Description	Page
1-Presidents Team	Mike Lincoln is not known for his Gettysburg address; Ian Kennedy did not ask Americans what they could do for their country; and Claudell Washington never famously said, "I cannot tell a lie." It is no lie, however, that this theme team consists of players whose last name or first name is an exact match to the last name of one of the U.S. Presidents.	17
2-Color Team	This team is not just (Bud) Black and (Bill) White; in fact, it goes beyond the primary colors. A team member must have some sort of color in his last name. If the player's name contains a color on a Crayola crayon, then we consider him for this team.	28
3-Food Team	Frank(s) and Bergers (Burgers), Bacon and Curry, Salmon and Roe and Ham and Fowl(er), these are just a few of my favorite food related player names that might be found on the All	37

Chapter - Theme	Description	Page
	Food Team.	
4-Occupation Team	A (Max) Butcher, a (Dusty) Baker but no John Candelaria maker. This team looks for player last names that reference an occupation that someone might have.	45
5-Animal Team	(Steve) Lyon, the Tigers and (Doug) Bair, oh my. This team looks for player names containing an animal.	53
6-Last Name Is Also a First Name Team	Whether you're Howard Frank or Frank Howard, you could be on this team containing players whose last name could also be used conventionally as a first name.	71
7-Flora Team	A (Pete) Rose by any other name would still smell as sweet and is still not in the Hall of Fame. That is why we plant our (Bob) Seeds so that they grow a strong (Charley) Root system and blossom into a (Homer) Bush, all the while making sure our (Norm) Branch is not covered with (Mike) Ivie. Flowers, trees or flora parts are what these players need to have in their names to be considered for this theme team.	77
8-Body Part Team	You have to have strong (Ricky) Bones and a lot of (Jim Ray) Hart, but most of all, you must use your (Dave) Brain to its fullest potential. To be included on this team, the player's name must contain a body part.	95
9-Financial Team	A (Brad) Penny for your thoughts. Personally, I'd rather put my (Don) Money in the (Ernie) Banks or a money market (Lee) Pfund so I can earn a good deal of (Dave) Cash. This team consists of players that have financial terms in	112

Chapter - Theme	Description	Page
	their names.	
10-Location Team	From (Kelly) Paris to (Gus) Britain, from (Al) Holland to (Clyde) Milan, from (Miguel) Cairo to (Frank) Brazil – though all-in-all, I'd rather take a rocket ship to the (Wally) Moon. This theme team includes players with well-known geographic locations in their names.	128
11-Smith Team	A team composed of players whose last name is Smith.	145
12-Jones Team	Not to be outdone by the Smiths, a team of players whose last name is Jones.	152
13-Gonzalez/ Martinez Team	The influence of the Latin player finds its way into a theme team with players whose last name is either Gonzalez or Martinez.	159
14-Weather Team	One might expect some (Bob) Hale coming in from the west that might change to some (JT) Snow. Don't expect any (Josh) Fogg, but there could be some (Rich) Gale force winds blowing in, leading to a big (Jake) Freeze. The forecast calls for a heavy dose of (Tim) Raines leading to a potential (Curt) Flood. It won't be long before (Ed) Summers is upon us, so have a (Harry) Bright day. This all (Roy) Weatherly team contains players whose names might be mentioned in a weather report.	165
15-Z Team	Its players may be used to appearing at the end of a conventional roster, but this team contains only Major Leaguers whose last name begins with the letter Z.	177
16-Automotive Team	Whether you drive a (Whitey) Ford, a (Jose) Mercedes or a (Jack) Bentley, each of us can do our part for the environment by not using (Pat)	184

Chapter - Theme	Description	Page
	Diesel in our (Chuck) Carr. This theme team consists of players whose names represent a car, truck or motorcycle brand, manufacturer, part or other automotive term.	
17-Berry/Bery Team	Phil Rizzuto never referred to me as a (Earl) Huckleberry. However, he once ate my (Darryl) Strawberry and (Dan) Quisenberry pie. Players that feature "berry" or "bery" somewhere in their names will comprise this delicious team.	205
18-What's in a name?	This is not really a theme team but a list of some of the best and worst names of Major League Baseball players, by position.	210
19-What's coming in Volume II	A look at potential themes for the next volume...	215

Preface

This book is a compilation of theme-based Major League Baseball all-star teams. Theme examples include the all-time U.S. Presidents team, consisting of the best Major League players who happen to have a name that matches the last name of a U.S. President, and the all-time color team, composed of players whose names contain one of the Crayola crayon colors.

The origin of this book can be traced to my love of sports, and in particular my fondness for baseball. Sports are a large part of my day-to-day life, whether it be coaching my kids' teams, watching professional or collegiate teams, or playing (or at least trying to play). When I get together with family and friends, no matter the topic du jour, we somehow wind up discussing sports – and especially baseball. For many individuals, it simply would not be possible to segue from the state of the economy, healthcare reform or how to defeat ISIS, to the merits (or lack thereof) of the designated hitter, the impact of PEDs on baseball's statistical records, the state of youth baseball in our town or how to use the bunt as a weapon in today's game, but somehow my family, friends and I consistently and effortlessly find ways to do so.

I have a few friends whom I have known since childhood, along with several from college, spanning over 30 years of companionship. In the time we have known each other, we have had ample opportunity to discuss all things baseball. In junior high and high school, we often passed the time trying to one-up each other with increasingly difficult trivia questions. Once these questions became too repetitive, we turned to more philosophical discussions comparing the best players across different eras and arguing over whether the Hall of Fame should be set up so that only a finite number of players be allowed to occupy it at one time (*e.g.*, to vote in someone new means you must also vote someone out). We have debated whether the Major League All-Star Game has passed its time and should be completely re-formatted as a U.S. versus the rest of the world game preceded by skills competitions such as the fastest man around the bases and the best and most accurate throwing arm. We have even pondered ways to speed up the pace of the game, including a pitch clock, limits on the number of times a pitcher and another player can confer on the mound, increasing the minimum number of batters a reliever must face from one to three, and starting innings almost immediately after the final out of the preceding inning.

Somehow, in the course of all our discussions – and I am not exactly sure why or when – we migrated to the topic of categorizing players by various themes such as those with a food-sounding name or a body part contained in the spelling or pronunciation of their names. Even today, it is not uncommon for me to be interrupted at work or awakened early in the morning by a friend with a proposal for a new team entry, such as insisting that Sixto (pronounced by my friend Ivan as "Six-toe") Lezcano should be a member of the Body Part Team. Clearly, a 50+ year-old man should have something better to do with his time than to dwell on such things and should further realize that "Sixto" is not a part of the body.

There was a time I thought these discussions of theme teams occurred strictly between me and my "seemingly normal on the outside but slightly disturbed on the inside" friends that I grew up with. However, over time, as I expanded my network of friends, I discovered that this fascination could be found outside of New Hyde Park and Great Neck, New York. As an avid ESPN viewer and listener to sports talk radio, I have even heard from time to time broadcasters like Tim Kurjian and Buster Olney refer to a potential theme team.

It is both comforting and worrisome to learn that many others have baseball discussions similar to those shared by me and my childhood friends. It wasn't, however, until my then six-year-old son noted that Randy Winn had a great name (since "Win" was in his name) and that he wanted Randy's team at the time (the New York Yankees) to "win" the game, that I began to seriously think about putting pen to paper to capture a comprehensive list of theme teams. And so, I started compiling the various themes that have been the topic of discussion over the years between me and my friends and gradually recreated the lists of players that we had included for each theme.

After compiling these lists, I started to wonder what names we missed during all those name games we played when we would go back and forth with one another until we were out of names or began to repeat them. I also started to wonder, within each given theme, what an all-star team would look like for that theme. Thus began the development of this book.

As I started to take a deeper dive into player names, the research began to take on a life of its own. Over time, I realized that this was more than a weekend project, since our command of the complete list of major league players had been fairly limited.

Because writing is not my full-time job, my pursuit to compile the all-time themed teams proceeded at a snail's pace. In fact, several years have passed since I first put together my initial lists. But thanks to support and inspiration from those who are noted in this book's dedication, I am happy to have finally completed Volume I and hope that it may lead to subsequent volumes. Perhaps it could even be expanded to include sports besides baseball, for as my youngest son has noted on more than one occasion, Nick Swisher would have been a great name for a basketball player.

If nothing else, I hope this book will add fuel those late-night discussions and help readers impress their own friends with such arcane knowledge as all the Major League Baseball players who share a surname with a U.S. president.

Introduction

To immortalize an all-star collection of name-based theme teams, I decided I needed to establish some basic ground rules to ensure a consistent approach (and avoid future late-night phone calls disputing my team selections). Following are my nine guidelines for assembling the all-time themed Major League Baseball teams:

1. No nicknames. The sport of baseball is rife with colorful nicknames which add to the fabric of the game. That said, to preserve the integrity of this team assembly exercise, I felt it important to eliminate nicknames in determining team eligibility. This step does reduce the pool of players available for certain themes – but not for others. For example, Hall of Fame pitcher Catfish Hunter is not eligible for the all-food team (Catfish) but still can be considered for the all-occupation team (Hunter is a great occupation, after all). Whitey Ford is not eligible for the all-color team (representing the color White) but is certainly on the short list for both the all-Presidents and all-automotive teams.
2. Keep it clean and avoid slang. This, too, was a tough rule to implement, but I hope that, as a result, this book can be enjoyed by the whole family (including my own). At the risk of disappointing my friends, Pete LaCock, Dick Pole, Josh Reddick and Paul Assenmacher will not appear on the all-time body part team, nor will Bobby Cox be named as that team's manager. Parents reading ahead may wish to omit discussion of those mentioned-for-humorous-purposes-but-disqualified names as well.
3. Use last name or first name but no middle names. It is okay to use a player's last or first name to categorize in a particular theme but no middle names. George Herman Ruth (aka the Babe) will not appear on any all-monster team (Herman Munster) should I decide to try assembling one. He will, however, be a prime candidate

to play on the all-time –my-last-name-is-also–a-first-name team (George and Ruth both are first names). This book will feature instances when only a last name is used to assign a player to a team but no instance when only a first name is used.

4. It is okay to use part of a player's name to qualify him for a particular theme team. For example, Mike Greenwell can be considered as a candidate for the all-color team, since the color "green" appears in his name and is clearly pronounceable.

5. The pronunciation of a player's name may or may not be relevant to his eligibility for a given themed team. More specifically, if the spelling of a player's name is an exact match for a particular theme, he qualifies for that theme's team regardless of how the player's name is pronounced. However, if the pronunciation of a player's name fits a particular theme, he qualifies for that theme's team even if his name's spelling does not fit. For example, Bartolo Colon (pronounced CO-LOAN) could be a candidate for the all-location team (*i.e.*, pronounced like the city of Cologne), as well as the all-body-part team (*i.e.*, the actual spelling of his last name, C-O-L-O-N, appears in the dictionary as a body part, albeit not one that's a fan favorite). Reid Nichols (pronounced NICKELS) is eligible for the all-financial team, as the pronunciation of his last name fits the financial theme (despite the fact that his last name's spelling does not support the fit).

6. Unless there are not enough players to fill a team, a name cannot be repeated. For example, Trot Nixon and Otis Nixon are both candidates for the all-Presidents team, since both their last names match that of former U.S. President Richard Nixon. However, since both have the same last name, only one can make the team (assuming there are enough candidates – pun intended – to fill the rest of the team's roster without using duplicate names). The obvious exception to this rule is where a team's theme requires the inclusion of players of

the same name (*e.g.*, the all-time Smith team necessitates that all of its players share the name Smith).
7. In filling team rosters, focus on players post 1900 where possible, so as to keep the game in the modern baseball era. That said, in discussing formation of team rosters, I also have attempted to identify all themed team candidates sourced from the pools of negro league players in the Hall of Fame even if they did not ever play in the Major Leagues, as well as Major League players prior to 1900. At the time of writing this book, I limited my team formations to Major League players who appeared through 2015, so future updates to this book may be required over time.
8. Full lineups. In selecting a team, the goal is to complete a roster which includes all position players (first base, second base, third base, shortstop, right field, center field, left field, catcher), a closer, and up to five starting pitchers. A designated hitter and relief pitchers also are considered. To be eligible for selection at a given position, a player must have recorded a put-out in at least one Major League game at that position, with the exception of the DH, where at least one at-bat at DH is required.
9. Find the best players among qualified candidates who are available for a given team. The first objective is to identify potential candidates by position. After compiling a list of theme-qualified players, it starts to get a bit subjective to select the best players at their respective positions, keeping in mind that sometimes the best overall players may be "competing" for the same spot on the team (by virtue of playing the same position) and thus may not be included. Since the goal is to have a unique name at each position (see rules 6 and 8), sometimes that will result in a marginal player making a team over a more acclaimed player simply because of the uniqueness of the lesser player's name. For example, in selecting the all-time Color Team, there are a lot of Greens, Whites, Browns and Blacks to choose from, but only a few Blues, one Lavender and one

Yellow. In this case, some great players will be left off the team simply because they have common names. Jim Lavender, for instance, was a pitcher for the Cubs and Phillies with a career 63 – 76 record. Many pitchers with the name Brown were simply better players. However, since Jim is the only Major Leaguer in history with the name Lavender, his chances of making a Color Team without players having duplicate names are greatly enhanced.

The above rules provide a layer of consistency for team assembly. Any additional theme-specific rules for a given team are outlined in the related chapter. While I don't expect these parameters to completely eliminate arguments among friends about team composition, I at least hope they will reduce the volume and duration of late-night calls. If not, call screening rules will be in effect!

I hope you have as much fun with my teams as I have had in discussing them over the years and assembling this first volume of all-time themed baseball teams.

If you would like to provide general feedback about this book, flag any omissions or errors you have identified, or share your own themed team or other suggestions for possible inclusion in a future book, please e-mail me at Paul@alltimethemedteam.com or tweet me at @themed_teams. I will do my best to respond, but please don't take it personally if I can't get back to you.

Thank you and enjoy!

Chapter One
The All-Time Presidents Team

Overview

Donald Trump was sworn in as the 45th President of the United States. However, the 45 U.S. Presidents reflect only 39 unique surnames (since two Bushes, two Harrisons, two Adams, two Johnsons and two Roosevelts have served, and Grover Cleveland, who served two nonconsecutive terms, is considered both the 22nd and the 24th U.S. President).

To be included on this team, the last or first name of the player must be an exact match to one of the 39 unique U.S. Presidential last names. In fielding this particular team, we forgo any name whose pronunciation (but not spelling) matches a former President's last name (*e.g.*, "Bush" qualifies but "Busch" does not).

Fun Facts

- Not all of the 39 unique Presidential last names have been represented among Major League Baseball players' last names over the years – in fact, the following 12 have not been represented: Trump, Obama, Eisenhower, Polk, Fillmore, Arthur, McKinley, Roosevelt, Taft, Coolidge, Truman or Reagan (although there have been several Regans).
- Of those 12 last names, however, five (Roosevelt, Arthur, Taft, Truman and McKinley) are represented among the *first* names of past or present Major Leaguers, leaving seven U.S. Presidential surnames (Trump, Obama, Eisenhower, Fillmore, Polk, Coolidge, Reagan)

- with no representation of any kind in Major League Baseball annals.
- Fewer than 700 of the 18,000+ people to play Major League Baseball offer an exact match by either first or last name to a U.S. President's last name.
- On a last name basis, Johnson is by far the most represented President's name in Major League Baseball history (over 100 Johnsons have played in the Majors). Arthur is by far the most popular first name match to a Presidential last name, given the more than 100 former or current players with the first name Arthur.
- After Arthur, Clinton is the most common Presidential last name represented as a first name in Major League Baseball history. This is followed very closely by Tyler, Grant, Wilson and Taylor.
- Some players share both their first name and last name with U.S. Presidents, such as Arthur Wilson, Washington Harrison and Tyler Johnson.
- Many players who qualify for the Presidents Team – with names like Washington, Lincoln, Cleveland, Jackson and Madison – also are candidates for the Location Team.
- There are seven unique Presidential surnames represented in the MLB Hall of Fame, including Carter, Ford, Johnson, Wilson, Grant, Taylor and Jackson, with multiple instances for each of Jackson, Johnson and Wilson.
- Adams, Pearce and Tyler represent the last names of players in the top 500 all-time MLB career batting average or ERA leaders.
- Pitcher is the most common position among candidates for the Presidents Team, and second base is the least common position.
- Hall of Fame pitcher Walter Johnson has the best career ERA (2.17) among all "Presidential" pitchers, followed by Babe Adams (2.76).
- Shoeless Joe Jackson has the best career batting average (.356) among "Presidential" players, followed by Hack Wilson (.307).

Qualified Player Counts
(In Alphabetical Order by President's Last Name)

President Last Name	Last Name Count	First Name Count	Total Count
Adams	33	0	33
Arthur	0	114	114
Buchanan	5	0	3
Bush	6	0	6
Carter	15	2	16
Cleveland	2	0	2
Clinton	2	9	11
Coolidge	0	0	0
Eisenhower	0	0	0
Fillmore	0	0	0
Ford	17	2	18
Garfield	1	0	1
Grant	7	8	15
Harding	1	1	2
Harrison	8	2	9
Hayes	10	0	10
Hoover	7	0	6
Jackson	39	4	38
Jefferson	3	3	6
Johnson	109	1	104
Kennedy	19	0	19
Lincoln	3	2	4
Madison	3	1	4
McKinley	0	1	1
Monroe	6	2	8
Nixon	6	0	6
Obama	0	0	0

President Last Name	Last Name Count	First Name Count	Total Count
Pierce	9	1	9
Polk	0	0	0
Reagan	0	0	0
Roosevelt	0	1	1
Taft	0	1	1
Taylor	49	5	51
Truman	0	1	1
Tyler	3	8	11
Van Buren	2	0	2
Washington	7	3	10
Wilson	72	7	75
Totals	444	179	623

Thought Process on Team Selection

While there are no shortages of player candidates for this team, the challenge in assembling it was finding the best players without repeating a name. Many quality Johnsons have played Major League Baseball, including Randy, Walter, Davey, Judy and Bob. Walter Johnson is arguably the best Presidential pitcher of all time. Similarly, Davey Johnson is arguably the best Presidential second baseman of all time. Yet, selecting any one of the deserving Johnsons requires omission of all the others (based on the guidelines for team assembly outlined above).

I decided the best approach to filling the team was to start with the pitching staff, see which great Presidential names stood out, and then do the same with the position players.

I started by reviewing the Hall of Fame and then expanded the list to include the top 500 career ERA leaders.

Whitey Ford, Walter Johnson and Randy Johnson are the only "Presidential" pitchers in the Hall of Fame. Whitey Ford seems like a lock but a decision had to be made between Walter and Johnson as to which candidate gets our vote. Team inclusion of one of the Hall of Fame Johnsons will eliminate many great position players such as Davey, Judy and Bob Johnson from consideration. From the top ERA list, I considered Babe Adams (career win/loss record of 194 – 140 and 2.76 ERA over 19 years) and Lefty Tyler (127 – 116 and 2.95 over 12 years) as possibilities. Since not many players share the names Adams or Tyler (there are more players with the first name Tyler than last name), I thought it prudent to rank Babe and Lefty against players with the same names. The only other relevant Adams (in my opinion) to have played in the Majors were third basemen Sparky and Bobby. The majority of other Tyler's are current players, and none has really distinguished himself at this time. As such, Babe and Lefty seemed like relatively easy Presidential pitcher selections on the basis of their lifetime stats – especially since their inclusion did not have much impact on the selection of the rest of the team.

Presidential position players from the Hall of Fame include: catcher Gary Carter; outfielders Reggie Jackson and Hack Wilson; and shortstop Travis Jackson. Also in the Hall of Fame are Negro League standouts Jud Wilson (3B/1B), Ben Taylor (1B), Judy Johnson (eliminated from consideration due to the Walter Johnson selection) and Frank Grant (a 19th-century player and therefore not a first choice, as the goal is to use modern players where possible). Consideration of players with the all-time best batting averages did not add any unique names, although I must note that Joe Jackson, who based on performance should be in the Hall of Fame, carries the 3rd-best all-time batting average.

From a position standpoint, Gary Carter seemed like a lock for the team, as he is the only Hall of Fame Presidential catcher, whereas the other players required some thought regarding the name/position trade-off (*e.g.*, battle of the Jacksons among Reggie, Travis and Joe; battle of the Wilsons between Hack and Jud).

Next, I tried to find the best Arthur, figuring that by doing so, I would eliminate a bunch of names from consideration, leaving me a much smaller pool of players to choose from to fill out the remainder of the team.

Surprisingly, none of the top 500 career batting average leaders had the first name Arthur, although three of the top 500 career ERA leaders had that first name. In 15 big-league seasons, Arthur Nehf compiled a career ERA of 3.20, winning 184 games while losing 120 (a .605 winning percentage, which is better than Hall of Famer Tom Seaver). He beat out Arthur Fromme and his 2.90 ERA but a rather pedestrian 80 – 90 record, as well as Bugs (Arthur) Raymond and his 2.49 ERA but 45 – 57 record.

Once I had the above framework for the team, I started to rank players by the remaining President names, noting their positions. This ultimately allowed me to make some position-based choices among players. In cases where there were few players for a particular name, I didn't bother ranking anyone, especially if I felt all the players for that name were marginal (the one Harding, for example, appeared in just one game), figuring I could always backtrack if I needed to fill a slot.

The rankings I came up with by name were as follows:

Buchanan: Brian (OF)

Bush: Donie (SS), Guy (P), Randy (OF)

Cleveland: Reggie (P)

Clinton: Lou (OF), Clint Hurdle (1B)

Grant: Grant Jackson (RP), Mudcat Grant (P)

Hayes: Von Hayes (OF, 1B, 3B), Charlie Hayes (3B)

Jefferson: Reggie (DH)

Kennedy: Adam (2B), Bob (OF)

Monroe: Craig (RF)

Nixon: Otis (LF), Trot (RF)

Pierce: Billy (P)

Taylor: Taylor Douthit (OF), Tony Taylor (2B, 3B), Ron Taylor (RP)

Washington: Claudell (OF), U.L. (SS), Ron (2B)

Using all of this information, I was able to make my final team.

The Final Team

The Pitching Staff

Starting Pitcher 1: Walter Johnson – Walter got the nod over Randy. Walter's 417 – 279 record and his career 2.17 ERA and 3,508 strikeouts gave him the statistical edge over Randy (303 – 166, 3.29 ERA although Randy led with 4,875 strikeouts). It is tough to argue against either pitcher but there was room for only one Johnson on the team. In 1909 – Walter in just his third year in the Majors was 13 – 25 with a 2.22 ERA. I guess he didn't have much run support.

Starting Pitcher 2: Whitey Ford – The Chairman of the Board was one of the easiest selections. He is clearly the best Ford ballplayer… and probably would have made a better President than Gerald. His .690 winning percentage (236 – 106) and six World Series rings make him stand out from other Fords.

Starting Pitcher 3: Billy Pierce – Pierce won almost as many games as Whitey Ford (211), although his winning percentage was inferior. Overall, Pierce was a 7-time all-star and posted a career record of 211 – 169 and an ERA of 3.27. With so few Pierces to play the game, he is by far the best Pierce in Major League history. His uniform was retired by the Chicago White Sox in 1987.

Starting Pitcher 4: Arthur Nehf. A match by first name, Nehf had a nice, albeit not spectacular, career. He does, however, have the distinction of being statistically the best overall pitching Arthur in Major League history. His lifetime stats include a 184 – 120 record and 3.20 ERA.

Starting Pitcher 5: Babe Adams. Charles "Babe" Adams is a lot like Arthur Nehf. He had a solid career, featuring a 194 – 140 record, close to 3,000 innings pitched and an ERA of 2.76 which ranks in the top 100 all-time.

Closer: Grant Jackson – He has the distinction of having both his first and last name matching a former U.S. President. I took Grant Jackson as a Grant in this case. He got the nod over Lefty Tyler simply because Lefty had so few relief appearances in his career and Grant was primarily a relief pitcher, albeit a setup man. Grant did compile 79 saves in his career, with a high of 14 in one season (1979).

The Outfield
Center Field: Hack Wilson. Wilson was no Hack and made the team as the best Presidential center fielder and the only one in the Hall of Fame. He got the nod over Willie Wilson. Willie had more career hits than Hack, but Hack's lifetime batting average of .307 and career .395 on-base percentage won him a spot on this team.

Right Field – Reggie Jackson. Filling the corner outfield was no easy task. The choice came down to two Jacksons -- Reggie in right or Shoeless Joe in left. While I think Joe Jackson belongs in the Hall of Fame, in the end, I decided that power was more valuable than batting average for this team. Either way, note that this selection of a Jackson for corner outfield eliminated Hall of Fame shortstop Travis Jackson from team consideration.

Left Field – Otis Nixon. My man Otis finished his career with a respectable .270 batting average and a .343 on-base percentage. While he was "not a crook," as his Presidential namesake may suggest, he did steal 620 bases over his career, ranking him 16th on the all-time list in that category.

The Infield and Designated Hitter

Catcher –Gary Carter is one of the easiest choices for this team but not without ramifications for the rest of the team. He is the only Hall of Fame catcher with the same last name of a U.S. President. Until we have a President Bench, Rodriguez or Piazza, Gary's place on this team is safe. However, choosing Gary Carter for catcher eliminates Joe Carter from consideration for the outfield. The bottom line here is that there have not been too many Presidential names represented in the catcher spot. The only other realistic option would have been to select Terry Kennedy.

First Base – Von Hayes. President Rutherford B. Hayes would have been proud of Von. Von played several positions, including outfield and third base, but first base was probably his best position. Hayes amassed 1,402 hits in his career, and despite a lifetime .267 batting average, he achieved a career on-base percentage of .354. A one-time all-star, Von got the nod over Charlie as the best Hayes of all time.

Second Base – Adam Kennedy. Adam suffered the dubious distinction of not being the best Kennedy, as he was a lesser player than Terry the catcher. However, filling second base was no easy task, given the small pool of Presidential players at that position. Adam's lifetime .277 batting average and .330 on-base percentage certainly were respectable.

Third Base – Tony Taylor. Taylor could very easily have been selected for second base and, similar to Kennedy, may not be the best Taylor to play in the Major Leagues. Arguably, the best Taylor was Taylor Douthit (unfortunately, for this team's purposes, an outfielder), who compiled a .291 batting average and .364 on-base percentage over his career, compared to Tony's .261 and .321 marks. However, Tony did collect 2,007 lifetime hits and was a two-time all-star.

Shortstop – Donie Bush. Owen Joseph "Donie" Bush made his debut in 1908 for the Detroit Tigers. A lifetime .250 hitter with a .356 on-base average and 404 stolen bases, Bush ranks in the top 100 all-time stolen base leaders.

DH – Reggie Jefferson. The DH has existed as a position only since 1973, so the pool of Presidential designated hitters was quite slim. Still, Reggie stood out as the best Jefferson. Although he played in only 680 games, primarily with the Boston Red Sox, he was a lifetime .300 hitter with a career .823 OPS (on-base percentage plus slugging percentage). By way of comparison, note that Hall of Famer Reggie Jackson's career .846 OPS was only marginally higher. Jefferson was elected DH since no other Jefferson's were worth considering. If we had been able to repeat names on this team, Jefferson probably would not have made it; instead, Reggie Jackson would have been selected as DH (which would have allowed Shoeless Joe Jackson to man the outfield).

Chapter Two
The All-Time Color Team

Overview

To come up with a list of colors, I went to Crayola. Referencing their list, I came up with a list of 85 unique, one-name colors, although two of the colors (gray and grey) I treated as identical and thus have a true count of 84 unique colors.

The complete list of colors used to find team members is as follows:

Almond	Chestnut	Indigo	Mulberry	Silver
Amethyst	Citrine	Jade	Olive	Smoke
Apricot	Copper	Jasper	Onyx	Soap
Aquamarine	Cornflower	Lavender	Orange	Strawberry
Asparagus	Cyan	Lemon	Orchid	Sunglow
Banana	Dandelion	Lilac	Peach	Tan
Beaver	Denim	Lime	Periwinkle	Tangerine
Bittersweet	Dirt	Lumber	Pink	Teal
Black	Eggplant	Magenta	Plum	Thistle
Blue	Emerald	Mahogany	Purple	Timberwolf
Blush	Fern	Maize	Red	Tulip
Brass	Fuchsia	Malachite	Rose	Tumbleweed
Brown	Gold	Manatee	Ruby	Violet
Canary	Gray	Maroon	Salmon	Weed
Cerise	Green	Melon	Sapphire	White
Cerulean	Grey	Mint	Scarlet	Wisteria
Cherry	Inchworm	Moonstone	Sepia	Yellow

It was obvious from the onset that many of the colors in the list, such as Sunglow, Inchworm and Moonstone, would be unlikely to have any representation in Major League Baseball. In fact, I initially was concerned that there might not be enough unique color names to fill a team, to the point where I might feel pressured to violate my self-imposed guideline not to duplicate names.

Before I started selecting the team in earnest, I compared the list of colors to the historical roster of Major Leaguers to make sure there would be an adequate list of players to complete my All-Time Color Team with a minimum of six pitchers (including one relief pitcher) and eight position players, with an optional ninth player to serve as a designated hitter. When I ran my comparison using a basic word search, many names appeared that I had not anticipated. For example, anyone named Fredrick appeared when I searched for the color red. So I decided I needed to establish some additional rules to keep the team as it was intended, as I did not think that the spirit of the exercise permitted a player named Fredrick should count as a representative of the color red. Similarly, I felt that the name Stanley should not be included for the color Tan.

I decided that to be included on this team, not only must the player's last or first name begin or end with the color but also the color must be clearly heard when the player's name is pronounced. For example, Mike Redmond is definitely a candidate representing the color red. However, Chris Truby is not a candidate to represent the color ruby, for even though the spelling of his name ends in the color "ruby," the word "ruby" is not independently heard when pronouncing the name "Truby."

I also determined to give priority to last names over first names in choosing players. If a color is represented by a last name, then I did not bother opening it up to available players whose first name contained the color, even if it meant omitting a more qualified player. This was particularly relevant to the colors olive and fern, as certain players' first names (*e.g.*, Oliver and Fernando) contain these colors.

Consistent with my standard rule for team selection, I considered no nicknames (sorry, Red Schoendienst).

Fun Facts

- A majority of the colors (64 out of 85) are not represented at all in Major League Baseball, leaving only 21 represented colors (or 20, since I combined gray and grey).
- Of the 20 represented colors, Brown is by far the most popular color surname. There have been over 80 Browns to play in the Majors, including Hall of Fame pitcher Mordecai "Three Fingers" Brown and Ray and Willard Brown from the Negro Leagues.
- There are almost as many Roses (seven) as Blacks (eight); excluding names that only contain Rose and Black (such as Rosen and Blackburn).
- There are more Salmons (four) than Lemons (three) (although I often put Lemon on my Salmon).
- Red is the most popular "colorful" nickname. Over 90 players have had the nickname Red, including Hall of Famers Red (Charles) Ruffing, Red (Albert) Schoendienst and Red (Urban) Faber.
- Seven of the 20 represented colors are represented by only one player, including Jasper (Hi Jasper – Starting/Relief Pitcher), Lavender (Jimmy Lavender – Starting/Relief Pitcher), Cherry (Rocky Cherry – Relief

Pitcher) and Yellow (Chief Yellow Horse – Relief Pitcher).
- Five (Lemon, Mint, Pink, Salmon, Silver) of the 13 colors having multiple representatives have fewer than six players representing the color in their names.
- Brown, White, Green and Lemon are the color names represented in the Hall of Fame, although White (Sol White) is for an executive (of the Negro Leagues), not a player.
- The top 500 ERA leaders of all time include Brown (Buster and Mordecai), White (Will, Ernie and Doc), Black (Dave) and Lavender (Jim).
- Buck Redfern (red and fern) is an example of a player having two colors represented in his name, but no player has three or more colors in his name.

Thought Process on Team Selection

Starting with the Hall of Fame yields players such as Mordecai Brown (Starting Pitcher), Hank Greenberg (1B) and Bob Lemon (Pitcher). Despite this colorful start, I needed to be cognizant that seven colors are represented by only one player each, and five other colors are represented by five or fewer players each – plus, I likely was going to have to confront some overlap and potential shortages at specific positions. Consequently, it was entirely possible that the team might not be able to contain any Hall of Famers. Still, it was my preference to select the best players, assuming I could still fill out the rest of the team, position by position.

It seemed to make the most sense to start by examining the best position player and pitcher for each color with little representation, then see what was left over before going to the Hall of Famers and the colors offering the most options (such as white, brown, black, blue, olive, gray/grey, rose, red, gold and tan).

Here is what I came up with:

Cherry: Rocky Cherry (RP, 1 – 4 win/loss record and 5.77 ERA)

Jasper: Henry Jasper (RP/SP, 10 – 12 and 3.48)

Lavender: James (SP/RP, 63 – 76 and 3.09)

Plum: Bill Plummer (C, .188 batting average and .267 on-base percentage)

Strawberry: Darryl Strawberry (OF)

Weed: Bert Weeden (pinch hitter with one career at-bat)

Yellow: Chief Yellowhorse (RP/SP, 8 – 4 and 3.93)

Lemon: Bob (SP), Chet (CF)

Mint: Greg Minton (RP, 59 -65 and 3.10)

Pink: George Pinkney (3B, infield)

Salmon: Tim Salmon (DH/1B)

Silver: Charlie Silvera (C)

When I looked at the above results, it was clear that filling the pitching spots was not going to be an issue, and the challenge was going to be selecting the position players, as I was not certain whether or not there would be enough unique colors to choose from. The potential to include Hall of Fame pitchers Bob Lemon and Mordecai Brown depended on the ability to fill the position players from the colors white, green, black, blue, gray/grey, gold, olive, pink, plum, rose, red, salmon, silver, strawberry and tan.

The position players who immediately stood out were Hank Greenberg (1B), Darryl Strawberry (RF) and Tim Salmon (DH). So, the question became whether or not I could fill catcher, second base, shortstop, third base, center field and left field with the remaining colors.

The Final Team

The Pitching Staff
Starting Pitcher 1 – Mordecai "Three Fingers" Brown. As a member of the Hall of Fame, he got the nod over Kevin Brown as the staff ace. Mordecai finished his career with a win/loss record of 239 – 130 and a microscopic 2.06 career ERA. On top of that, he accumulated 49 saves.

Starting Pitcher 2 – Bob Lemon. Bob is also a Hall of Famer and made the team over center fielder Chet Lemon. Bob finished his career with a win/loss record of 207-128 and a 3.23 ERA. Bob is also known for taking over for Billy Martin as manager of the New York Yankees and guiding them to a World Series title in 1998.

Starting Pitcher 3 – Frank Tanana. Representing the color tan, Frank compiled more wins (240) than any other color-named pitcher. In a career that spanned 20 years, Frank struck out 2,773 batters, ranking him 21st of all time in that category.

Starting Pitcher 4 – Jim Lavender. As the only player named Lavender in Major League history, Jim partially falls into the category of "Hey, we need the dudes." Without repeating colors and without having an impact on the selection of position players, Jim was able to make this team. While his career win/loss record of 63 – 76 was not all-star caliber, his career ERA of 3.09 does rank him in the top 500 of all-time.

Starting Pitcher 5 – Bud (Harry) Black. Bud got to round out this colorful staff based on his career 121 – 116 win/loss record and 3.84 lifetime ERA, and the main fact that there were no great position players impacted by Bud's selection at pitcher. Vida Blue was omitted, as discussed below, because his inclusion would have an adverse impact on filling the position players.

Closer – Greg Minton. Representing the color mint, Greg owned the distinction of having the most career saves (150) of any of the available colors. His 15-year MLB career and unique color name added to his credentials for team selection.

The Outfield
Center Field – Darryl Strawberry. Although primarily a right fielder, Darryl did play some center. Chet Lemon would

have been the choice here had I not used Lemon on the pitching staff.

Right Field – Al Oliver. I went with Al Oliver to represent the color olive. Al was a great hitter, as evidenced by his career .303 batting average and 2,743 lifetime hits. These numbers are arguably Hall of Fame caliber.

Left Field – Pete Rose. The all-time leader in hits and baseball bets, Pete represents the color rose. Pete was a candidate for several positions but fits nicely in left field. Unfortunately, his selection did adversely impact the infield by eliminating third baseman Al Rosen team consideration.

The Infield and Designated Hitter

Catcher – Mike Redmond. Although Mike was primarily a backup catcher, he does sport a lifetime .287 batting average and .342 on-base percentage. Most "Red" Major Leaguers get their color from nicknames and thus were not options to make this All-Color Team. Mike is one of the few players with the color red actually in his name and has respectable offensive numbers for the catching position – and thus fits on this team.

First Base – Hank Greenberg. Representing the color green, this was the easiest selection. If this Hall of Famer were playing today, he would be making a lot of green. A lifetime .313 hitter with a .412 on-base percentage, Hank combined power (331 home runs) with a great eye. He finished with more walks than strikeouts and is clearly the best "Green" of all time.

Second Base – Frank White. While Frank may not be the best player named White to play the game, he is the best second baseman by that name. His selection boiled down to a small pool of second basemen. Bill White and Hall of Famer Deacon White are arguably the best infielders named White. But Bill had the misfortune of playing the same position as Hank Greenberg and Deacon had the misfortune of playing a position represented by a larger pool of potential All-Color Team members. Roy White has similar lifetime numbers to Bill, but there were more outfielders to choose from, so it was easier to omit Roy and the other available Whites. In the end, Frank won out by playing the right position.

Shortstop – Tony Fernandez. Representing the color fern, Tony got the nod over pitcher Sid Fernandez and third baseman George Pinkney. And with over 2,000 hits, Tony stood out among the "colorful" shortstops.

Third Base - Ossie Bluege. Ossie may not be the best "Blue" to have played in the Majors and probably is not the best "colorful" third baseman (that distinction goes to Al Rosen). First baseman Lu Blue and Pitcher Vida Blue are arguably more worthy choices for the team. Lu unfortunately played first base (and ranks behind Hank Greenberg). Vida Blue would have been the third pitcher behind Mordecai Brown and Bob Lemon, but some juggling was required to fill out the rest of the team. So apologies to Vida Blue – and to Al Rosen, who was eliminated with the selection of Pete Rose.

DH – Tim Salmon. Tim was a solid Major League player – and clearly the best named Salmon – having compiled a lifetime .282 batting average and .385 on-base percentage, together with 299 career home runs. His selection eliminated shortstop candidate Chico Salmon from consideration.

Chapter Three
The All-Time Food Team

Overview

Baseball names have included various food categories, such as: appetizers (*e.g.*, Pate), entrées (*e.g.*, Veal, Fish, Ham), side dishes (*e.g.*, Fries, Beans), condiments (*e.g.*, Mayo, Butter, Creamer), spices and seasonings (*e.g.*, Salt, Pepper, Curry), fruits and vegetables (*e.g.*, Leek, Pear, Lemon, Cherry, Apple), places to eat (*e.g.*, Deli), desserts (*e.g.*, Pie, Carmel), beverages (*e.g.*, Brew, Beer, Wine, Sherry); Oats & Grains used in cooking (*e.g.*, Wheat, Oat) and food/cooking terms (*e.g.*, Chow, Brown, Bake).

To be included on this team, the spelling or pronunciation of a player's surname needs to contain a food or drink (sorry, everyone with the first name Frank and to Marlin Stuart as these individuals are excluded) that one would typically consume or an ingredient that one would use to make a food or drink. Although names which reflect food-related terms, such as Brown and Bake, are fun to reference, they are not used for this team. Sorry friends, but Phil Rizzuto does not pass as Risotto and nobody is going to mistake George Sisler for the owner of the Sizzler restaurant chain.

Fun Facts

- Over 100 unique surnames, representing more than 225 players, contain some reference to food.
- While there have been no Fish, at least 20 Fishers have played Major League Baseball, as well as four Salmon, three Trout, seven Bass and three Herring.

- Fish is the most popular entrée found in players' surnames, with the most common occurrence found in the name Fisher. This does not even include MLB's offerings of types of fish such as Trout, Bass, Salmon, Garr (technically, the fish species is spelled "gar") and Haddock, and seafood such as Roe and Crab.
- No Sardines – but two guys named Sardinha played in the Majors.
- When it comes to surnames, Burgers are slightly more popular than Franks. The most common "burger" player name comes from the pronunciation of Berger. "Frank" surnames include Frank, Franco and Francona.
    - Franks include:
        - Frank (Charlie and Mike)
        - Franks (Herman)
        - Frankhouse (Fred)
        - Not to mention numerous Franklins and Francos
    - Beans include:
        - Bean: (Belve, Bill, Colter, Joe)
        - Beane (Moneyball's own Billy)
        - Lima (Jose)… (OK, it's pronounced Leema but spelled like the bean!)
    - Burgers include:
        - Berger (Boze, Brandon, Clarence, Heinie, Joe, Johnny, Tun, Wally)
        - Bamberger (George, Hal)
- The Hall of Fame is well represented by food names covering a variety of categories, including:
    - Cooking Terms: Brown, bake (Baker)
    - Appetizers: Cobb (as in cobb salad or corn on the cob)
    - Fruits & Vegetables: Lemon
    - Side Dishes: Rice (I know it is also a grain)
    - Oats & Grains: Wheat

- Several colors represented in the All-Time Color Team are also potential candidates for the All-Time Food Team, including Wheat, Lemon, Cherry, Strawberry, Olive, Salmon and Mint.
- Baseball has had its Salt (Jarrod Saltalamacchia, Jack Saltzgaver) and Pepper (Bob, Don, Laurin, Ray)
- There have been nine different players named Rice, two of whom are in the Hall of Fame (Sam and Jim).
- Baseball has had its share of fruits, to wit: three Lemons (Bob, Chet, and Jim), one Lemonds (Dave) and a Lemon Jello (Mark Lemongello); one Strawberry (Darryl), nine Berry(s), one Cherry (Rocky), one Grape (Rick Grapenthin).
- While there's many a Pear contained in names like Pearce and Pearson, there has only been one with the name Pears (Frank). There are no Plums, but there was one Plummer (Bill).
- Even excluding players with the first name Oliver, Olive is an extremely popular fruit, with nine Olivers, an Oliveras and an Oliveros among player surnames.
- Brown is the most popular food/cooking term (although cooking terms are not included as part of this theme team).

Thought Process on Team Selection

As is the case with all of my team assemblies, I started with the Hall of Fame. This yielded the following names:

Ty Cobb (Salad) – Center Field

Harmon Killebrew (Brew being a beverage made by brewing) – First Base

Bob Lemon – Starting Pitcher

Jim Rice – Left Field

Sam Rice – Right Field

Zack Wheat – Left Field

This yield surpassed my expectations, as it provided me with a complete outfield, a corner infielder and a starting pitcher. The only meaningful decision here – and not much of one – was which Rice to select. Since I already had a Hall of Fame food left fielder in Zach Wheat, Sam Rice got the nod over Jim Rice based solely on position. This resulted in a very healthy outfield consisting of grains and a type of salad.

This left me in search of four starting pitchers, a catcher, third baseman, shortstop, second baseman, closer and DH.

For a closer, two names immediately stood out – John Franco and Dan Quisenberry. Remembering Quisenberry's old battery mate led me to Darryl Porter, an excellent hitting catcher. I'm not sure I would choose a dark beer like a Porter to wash down my (Quisen) berries, but I needed to keep an open mind.

I then set out to identify potential middle infielders. In searching through the list of the top career hitters, I came across several food names, including Ralph Garr (again, as in "gar" the type of fish), Wally Berger, Julio Franco and Tim Salmon (from the Color Team). Ralph Garr was an outfielder and gar is not a very tasty fish (as far as I'm concerned), so he was not a likely fit. I like burgers, so I hoped to add one to the team, but Wally

Berger as a first baseman/outfielder was not a great positional fit, especially with Harmon Killebrew as a Hall of Fame first baseman. Julio Franco, on the other hand, played both middle infield positions, so I kept him on my short list and figured I would need to decide between Julio and John as the best Franks to serve with this team.

Similarly, I scanned through the top wins and ERA leaders of all time. A few notable names from this list included Charlie Root (although I felt calling a root a food might be pushing it but certainly something that you cook with), David Cone (a nice dessert), Dizzy Trout, Andy Coakley (as in "Have a Coke and a Smile"), Joe Berry, Heine Berger, Tiny Bonham, Al McBean (good dish with a Frank), Earl Yingling (perhaps Yingling is better than a Porter).

Other food names that also stood out were Al Olive(r), Darryl Strawberry, Greg Mint(on), Dick Groat (groat being a grain), Scott "Dinner" Rol(en), Ralph Kress (cress being an edible herb) and my personal favorite Tom "The Candy Man" Candiotti.

The Final Team

The Pitching Staff
Starting Pitcher 1 – Bob Lemon. Having already made the All-Time Color Team as the number two starter, Bob moves up one spot to be the ace of the All-Time Food Team. Bob finished his career with a win/loss record of 207-128 and a 3.23 ERA and managed the New York Yankees to a World Series title in 1998.

Starting Pitcher 2 – Dizzy Trout. I picked Dizzy over Steve Trout. With a career record of 170 – 161 and a 3.23 ERA, Dizzy may not be the prototypical number 2 starter. However, we slot him in at number 2 because we felt Trout should be served under Lemon. By the way, give Mike Trout a few more years of service, and we surely will be rethinking the selection of this particular Trout dish (though as an outfielder, of course).

Starting Pitcher 3 – David Cone. By talent alone, Cone makes sense as our number two starter, but he dropped to number three here because I felt he should come after an entrée like Trout. Cone finished his career with a 194 – 126 record and a 3.46 ERA.

Starting Pitcher 4 – Tom Candiotti. Candy and Cone just seemed like they go together, am I right? Tom also has the distinction of having a salad-based middle name (Caesar). He finished with a 151-164 record and a 3.73 ERA. While several other food-named pitchers had better ERAs, I ultimately went with longevity and the desire to have a knuckleballer on the staff.

Starting Pitcher 5 – Firpo Marberry. Marberry was a versatile pitcher who finished his career with a 148-88 record and a 3.64 ERA, while also earning 101 saves. His inclusion as a Berry meant Dan Quisenberry was left off the team.

Closer – John Franco. In the end, I picked Franco over Quisenberry and Greg Minton. Franco ranks fourth all-time in saves, with 424 (versus 244 for Quisenberry and 150 for Minton). While Quisenberry had a marginally superior ERA (2.76 vs 2.89), the combination of Franco's far superior saves number, longevity of 19 years and the fact that we wanted a

Frank earned him the spot. Of course, his inclusion meant Julio Franco was omitted.

The Outfield

Center Field – Ty Cobb. A Hall of Famer with the highest all-time batting average (.366), ninth in on-base percentage (.430) and second in hits (4,189). This was no contest unless you don't consider Cobb a food (but I do).

Right Field – Sam Rice. Sam got the nod over Jim Rice because Sam was a natural right fielder. With 2,987 career hits and a .322 career batting average, he was extremely worthy of the selection.

Left Field – Zach Wheat. Zach joins Bob Lemon as another member of the Color Team to make it on the Food Team. A .317 lifetime batting average and 2,884 career hits are a welcome addition to any team.

The Infield and Designated Hitter

Catcher – Darryl Porter. Darryl Porter makes the team as a beverage (dark beer). He finished his career with a .247 batting average and a .354 on-base percentage. His best year was 1979, when he batted .291 with a .421 OBP and .905 OPS.

First Base – Harmon Killebrew. How fitting to take a brew after a porter. Of course, this brew truly packs a wallop, with his Hall of Fame career accentuated by 573 career home runs (without the aid of PEDs, it would appear) and .376 career on-base percentage.

Second Base – Ray Durham. I picked this ham over Granny Hamner and Mike Hampton. Ray might be the best overall ham in any event, but playing second base certainly increased his value. With 2,054 career hits and a .352 lifetime on-base percentage, Durham certainly makes for a tasty middle infielder.

Shortstop – Dick Groat. For those wondering exactly what a groat is, it is hulled kernels of oats, buckwheat or barley. For this team, I decided to pick a grain over an herb (Ralph Kress). From 1952 to 1967, Dick played in 1,929 games. At a time when shortstop was not known as an offensive position, Dick managed to amass 2,138 career hits and had a .286 career batting average. In today's terms, he would be worth over $10 million a year.

Third Base – Scott Rolen. Since we have some Wheat on the team, we might as well get a "Roll" out of it with Scott Rolen. Ruling out nicknames meant Pie Traynor was not available and ruling out use of food/cooking terms also omitted Frank Baker. Arguably in the top 20 third basemen of all time, Scott is the only one of the top tier who fits the food category based on our stringent rules... until, of course, a food is named "the Schmidt" (which would allow us to select Mike).

DH – Al Oliver. Al Oliver made this team over his fellow member of the Color Team Tim Salmon. This was not an easy choice, however. While Al has a significant edge in hits (2,743 to 1,674) and batting average (.303 to .282), Salmon has the edge in home runs (299 to 219) and on-base percentage (.385 to .344). Oliver's longevity and ability to play all outfield positions in his prime ultimately led me to select him over Salmon. And with a Trout on the pitching staff, enough fish already!

Chapter Four
The All-Time Occupation Team

Overview

Baseball names have encompassed many a great occupation. There have been Bakers, Hunters, a Singer, a Boss and – a personal favorite – a Bard. This team includes players whose last names represent, either in spelling or pronunciation, some sort of occupation that a person might have (or want).

Fun Facts
- The Hall of Fame is stocked with both well-known and esoteric occupations, including a Baker (Frank), Carter (Gary), Cooper (Andy), Dean (Dizzy), Hunter (Catfish), Page (Satchel Paige), Speaker (Tris), Tailor (Ben Taylor), Ward (John), Smith (Ozzie), Tinker (Joe) and Weaver (Earl).
- While there are many with the nickname Doc and some actual doctors, there has never been a Major Leaguer with the last name Doctor or who is a lawyer. However, there has been a Judge.
- Baker is the most popular occupational name, borne by at least 29 former and current players.
- Major League Baseball has had its share of royalty, with Kings, Queens, Knights, Bishops, Lords and an Earle.
- Tris Speaker ranks as the top occupational hitter, with 3,514 hits and a career .345 batting average.
- Ward Taylor Miller holds the distinction of having his first, middle and last names all represent occupations.

Thought Process on Team Selection

Five occupational pitchers are in the Hall of Fame, including Andy Cooper, Dizzy Dean, Catfish Hunter, Satchel Paige and Hilton Smith. Andy Cooper (a Negro Leagues standout) never played in the Majors, so it was not a given that he was going to make the team, despite his Hall of Fame pedigree. Satchel Paige, on the other hand, did pitch in the Majors, albeit towards the end of his career. Reviewing available Negro League records and independent accounts certainly factored into my thinking regarding Paige.

Occupational position players in the Hall of Fame include Ben Taylor at first base; Gary Carter at catcher; Joe Tinker, Ozzie Smith and John Ward at shortstop; Tris Speaker in center field; and Frank Baker and Pie Traynor at third base, with Earl Weaver as the manager.

As you can see, the Hall of Fame reflects a fair share of occupations, but with significant overlap, including two Smiths, two third basemen and multiple shortstops.

Gary Carter (a carter being someone who drives a cart) and Tris Speaker stood out as great players with no overlap and therefore seemed like sure hires for the team.

With no second basemen and no corner outfielders represented in the Hall of Fame, I started looking at potential hires for these positions. Unfortunately, there is no such occupation as a Hornsby. If only Rogers' surname were Hornblower, then we would have something. Undaunted by this setback, I looked at various all-time rankings for second basemen and came across a couple of occupations in Max Bishop and Tony Taylor.

Similarly, I found Larry Walker and Dave Parker among the all-time greats in right field.

Left field proved to be a bit more problematic. One name that I came up with was the great Joe Carter. Of course, including him on the team would be in conflict with selecting another carter in Gary Carter.

To be safe, I looked back at other notable catchers to come up with Darrell Porter and Walker Cooper (whose first name and surname are both occupations).

I also began to look at some great players in the top of the all-time batting lists. During this process, I found a Judge (Joe), a Miller (Bill Mueller), a Butler (Brett), a Parker (Dave), a Gardner (Larry), and a Wit (Whitey Witt), although I'm not sure a Wit is a paying occupation. I also found several Smiths and several Walkers.

I had to rule out some occupational classifications – for instance, Leach (Freddy), as I felt that it was not something you really got paid to be. I also ruled out Stewart, which I deemed not close enough in pronunciation to Steward. In addition, I ruled out Hack as an occupation.

Finally, I looked for potential closers with Lee Smith, Mike Marshall and Jim Brewer all in the running for a spot.

With my short list by position, I was ready to select the final team.

The Final Team

The Pitching Staff

Starting Pitcher 1 – Satchel Paige. Paige's Major League statistics were not Hall of Fame worthy. He finished his MLB career with a 28-31 record and a 3.29 ERA in just 476 innings. However, he debuted in the Majors at age 42, after a long, distinguished career in the Negro Leagues. Satchel also has the distinction of being the oldest player ever to appear in a Major League game when, at age 59, he pitched three innings for the Kansas City Athletics. The great baseball historian and father of sabermetrics, Bill James, wrote of Satchel: "What you have, in Satchel Paige, is a great fastball, great control, a tremendous change, a great understanding of how to pitch, intelligence, determination, absolute composure—and a forty-year career… I think that Satchel deserves to rank, with Cy Young, Lefty Grove, and Walter Johnson, as the guys that you talk about when you're trying to figure out who was the greatest that ever lived." If he was good enough for Bill James, then he certainly is good enough to head our team as our uniformed employee (a page).

Starting Pitcher 2 – Catfish Hunter. Jim Catfish Hunter won 224 games (against 166 losses) and finished his career with a 3.26 ERA and one Cy Young award. He was an eight-time MLB All-Star and won five World Series rings. As a member of the Hall of Fame, he was a lock to make our team as a professional Hunter.

Starting Pitcher 3 – Dizzy Dean. The Dean of our team is none other than Hall of Famer Jay "Dizzy" Dean. Injury cut short Dean's career, in which he won 150 games against 83 losses and compiled a 3.02 ERA. Dean's 1934 season was one for the ages. He went 30 -7 with a 2.66 ERA and seven saves. He led the league that year in wins and strikeouts and was second in ERA and saves.

Starting Pitcher 4 – John Tudor. I settled on the teacher (Tutor) based on his 117-72 record and lifetime 3.12 ERA.

Starting Pitcher 5 – Silver King. This was my most difficult choice and one where I definitely had to take some liberties. My two choices came down to Hall of Famer Andy Cooper and pre-1900 pitcher Silver King. Neither candidate quite fit my rules-based model, but in the end I opted for royalty, if for no other reason than Silver King compiled MLB statistics. Unfortunately for Andy Cooper, the Negro Leagues were often void of statistics. I'm particularly fond of Silver King's 1888 season, where he went 45 -21 with 585 innings pitched and a 1.64 ERA.

Closer – Mike Marshall. I picked Mike Marshall over Lee Smith, Stu Miller and Jim Brewer. The omission of a Smith at closer probably bodes well for another position player named Smith. Mike Marshall is 50th all-time in saves (188). While this trails well behind Lee Smith's 478, Marshall still was an outstanding reliever at a time when "closers" were often called upon to pitch several innings. This is best illustrated by his 1974 season, when Marshall logged 208 innings in 106 appearances. In his 14-year career, Marshall recorded over 100 innings pitched in a season six times and 99 innings pitched twice.

The Outfield

Center Field – Tris Speaker. In this case, the Butler did not do it. We picked Tris the orator Speaker over the servant Brett Butler. Tris ranks fourth all-time in batting average(.345) and ninth all-time in on-base percentage (.428). His 3,515 hits rank him fifth all-time.

Right Field – Larry Walker. I selected a Walker over a car Parker (Dave Parker). Larry Walker and Dave Parker have similar statistics, but Larry edges Dave in two important offensive categories: batting average (.313 vs. .290) and on-base percentage (.400 vs. .339). Larry also had more home runs (383 vs. 339), but I attribute that in large part to Larry's playing a significant portion of his career in Colorado. Dave had the advantage in career hits (2,712 vs. 2,160). While Dave was considered the superior defender, it was the gap in on-base percentage that ultimately led me to select Larry.

Left Field – Bing Miller. Left field was perhaps my toughest choice, with what seemed like a scarcity in occupational players. While I felt Joe Carter was a worthy candidate, I did not want to eliminate another Hall of Famer (catcher Gary Carter). In the end, I selected Miller. Miller had a career .311 batting average and had the distinction of drawing more walks than strikeouts (383 vs. 340). He was extremely versatile, having played all outfield positions, and was dubbed as "Old Reliable."

The Infield and Designated Hitter

Catcher – Gary Carter. Hall of Famer Gary Carter was an easy choice for this team. "The Kid" is often in the conversation as one of the top 10 catchers of all-time, and his 324 home runs,

2,092 career hits and overall defensive presence behind the plate made him our top choice as occupational catcher.

First Base – Joe Judge. First base was another tough position, but my verdict was to select a Judge over a Cooper (Cecil). I will let you be the judge, but here was the comparison of hits (2,352 vs. 2,192), on-base percentage (.378 vs. .337), home runs (71 vs. 241), OPS (.798 vs. .803) and stolen bases (213 vs. 89).

Second Base – Max Bishop. Since I had a King on the team, why not a Bishop? I selected Max Bishop over Tony Taylor. In a career that spanned from 1924 to 1935, Max played for the Philadelphia Athletics and Boston Red Sox. By today's standards, he would be considered a "moneyball" player, with a career .423 on-base percentage and .271 batting average. In 1,338 career games, the Bishop amassed 1,216 hits along with 1,153 walks.

Shortstop –Ozzie Smith. Shortstop was a position with several options, including a Tinker (Joe Tinker) and a Ward (John Ward). However, the Wizard of Oz stood out as one of the top all-around shortstops.

Third Base – Pie Traynor. This position posed another tough choice. I selected Pie over the Baker (or should I say a trainer over a baker). Both Hall of Famers, it came down to Pie having slightly better statistics and being deemed a better fielder. Pie had a career .320 batting average (vs. .307 for Baker) and amassed more hits (2,416 vs. 1,838).

DH – Frank Baker. I took the easy way out on this one and selected Hall of Famer Frank Baker. While he played before the existence of the DH, a Baker surely will keep the team well fed and ready to play. Baker's .307 lifetime batting average is the highest among the remaining available occupational players and his inclusion in the Hall of Fame meant we needed to find a place for him.

Bonus Selection – The Manager

Earl Weaver -- This team seemed like it needed a manager, and there can be no better occupationally named manager than Earl Weaver… especially since Stengel is not an occupation that I'm aware of.

Chapter Five
The All-Time Animal Team

Overview

Professional baseball has featured a lot of animalistic nicknames over the years, including Catfish, Goose, Birdie/Bird and Moose, just to name a few. But to be included on this team, the pronunciation of a player's surname must contain some kind of an animal.

Close matches like Goslin (for Gosling) do not qualify for this team.

Animal breeds, such as Collie as found in Collier, are acceptable only if the animal name is identifiable in the pronunciation of the surname. As such, Beard (as in the facial hair) does not qualify for Bear, but Baird does qualify.

While it is by no means an exhaustive list, I selected the team from the following list of animals:

Ant	Cow	Goose	Lemming	Pika
Alligator	Coyote	Gosling	Lemur	Pike
Armadillo	Crab	Gopher	Leopard	Poodle
Baboon	Crane	Gorilla	Liger	Possum
Badger	Crocodile	Grasshopper	Lion	Puffin
Barb	Cuscus	Grouse	Lizard	Pug
Barnacle	Dalmatian	Guppy	Lobster	Puma
Bass	Deer	Hamster	Lynx	Quail
Bat	Dhole	Hare	Macaw	Rabbit
Beagle	Dingo	Harrier	Maltese	Rat

Bear	Discus	Hawk	Manatee	Roach
Beaver	Dodo	Hen	Mandrill	Robin
Bengal	Dog	Heron	Mastiff	Salmon
Bird	Dolphin	Hog	Mole	Shepherd
Bison	Donkey	Horse	Molly	Skunk
Bongo	Duck	Human	Mongoose	Stork
Booby	Dunker	Husky	Mongrel	Sloth
Buffalo	Eagle	Hyena	Moose	Swan
Bull	Eel	Ibis	Morgan	Tang
Caiman	Emu	Iguana	Moth	Tapir
Calf	Falcon	Impala	Mouse	Tiger
Camel	Ferret	Insect	Mule	Trout
Caracal	Finch	Jackal	Newt	Turkey
Cardinal	Fish	Jaguar	Ocelot	Vulture
Cat	Fisher	Kakapo	Olm	Wallaby
Cheetah	Fly	Kangaroo	Otter	Wasp
Chicken	Fox	Kingfisher	Ox	Weasel
Chick	Frog	Kiwi	Panther	Wolf
Cock	Gar	Kudu	Parrot	Wren
Collie	Gecko	Lamb	Peacock	Yak
Coral	Giraffe	Lark	Penguin	Zebra
Cougar	Goat	Leach	Pig	

Fun Facts

- The Hall of Fame has its share of animals, including two foxes (Nellie Fox and Jimmie Foxx), one lion (Ted Lyons), a hen (Ricky Henderson), a cock (Mickey Cochrane), a robin (Brooks, Frank and Jackie Robinson), a lark (Barry Larkin) and a breed of horse (Joe Morgan).
- Jackie Robinson leads all animalistic players with a lifetime .311 batting average.

- Fish or Fisher is the most common animal name found in baseball, including least 28 MLB players named Fisher or Fischer. This figure does not even count players with names representing a species of fish, like Garr (gar is the fish) and Trout.
- The lion is the most popular of the big cats in baseball, with 15 occurrences (in the form of Lyon and Lyons).
- While Cat can be found in several surnames, the pronunciation of it can only be found in a few names, notably Frank Catalanatto, Tom Catterson, Ray Katt and Bob Katz.
- While many fans may disagree in a figurative sense, no Dogs have played in the Majors, but a couple of dog breeds are represented in the names Shepard/Shepherd and Collier (Collie).
- Wolves are one of the most popular animalistic names, with at least 18 players named Wolf, Wolff, Wolfe and a personal favorite, Wolfgang. Wolf nudges out fox (with 17 players) covered by the name Fox, Foxx and Foxen.
- In addition to the "ox" found in Fox, there have been two players with the name Ox (in Oxspring and Oxley).
- Gar is the most popular fish name, thanks in part to the numerous players named Garcia and Gardner. Less popular fish names include Bass (nine), Salmon (four) and Trout (three).
- Although several players have had the nickname Ducky, only two ducks (both with the name Duckworth) have played in the Majors.
- Beyond the several players who have had the nickname Goose, there has been one goose name (Greg Goossen) and one Gosling (Mike Gosling).

- Three Birds and one Birdsall have played in the Majors, in addition to several Byrds (Jeff, Jim, Paul, Sammy) and a Byrdak (Tim). In addition, there have been cardinals (Jose Cardenal and Conrad Cardinal) and finches (Joel Finch, Bill Fincher). While only one chick (Travis Chick), there has been – pardon my French – several cocks (including Jim Cockman and Alan Cockrell) to play in the Majors. Still, hen is the most popular kind of chicken thanks to the surnames Henderson and Hendricks. There's been only one eagle (Bill Eagle) although many a wren thanks to many a surname beginning with "ren.". Other represented bird species include crane, peacock, crow, chick and hawk.

Thought Process on Team Selection

The Hall of Fame provides three second base candidates: (Joe) Morgan (breed of horse), Jackie Robin(son) and Nellie Fox. There is a lion for a pitcher in Ted Lyons and a Hen(derson) for left field, a Robin(son) for third base in Brooks and another Robin(son) for right field in Frank. With a second Fox at first base (Jimmie Foxx) and three Robins, some Hall of Famers was sure to be omitted. The steepest challenge was choosing which Robinson to use, especially since there is no positional overlap with Brooks and Frank. While I felt like I couldn't go wrong with any of the Hall of Fame second basemen in isolation, selecting Joe Morgan would maximize the number of Hall of Famers who could be selected for the team. Where no positional or name overlap existed, as was the case at catcher (Mickey Cochrane) and pitcher (Ted Lyons), these players seemed like locks to make the team.

To search for the remainder of the club, I decided to make a list of candidates by animals not found in the Hall of Fame and by position, then from within each animal and each position, find the top players to make a short list.

My complete list of potential remaining players included the following:

Player Name	Position	Years Played	Animal
Joe Antolick	C	1944	Ant
John Antonelli	3B	1944-1945	Ant
Johnny Antonelli	P	1948-1961	Ant
Matt Antonelli	2B	2007-2009	Ant
Bill Antonello			Ant
Walter Barbare	SS	1914-1922	Barb
Red Barbary	PH	1943	Barb
Jap Barbeau	3B	1905-1910	Barb
Dave Barbee	LF	1926-1932	Barb
Brian Barber	P	1995-1999	Barb
Steve Barber	P	1960-1974	Barb
Steve Barber	P	1970-1971	Barb
Turner Barber	LF	1915-1923	Barb
Frank Barberich	P	1907-1910	Barb
Bret Barberie	2B	1991-1996	Barb
Jim Barbieri	OF	1966	Barb
George Barnicle	P	1939-1941	Barnacle
Dick Bass	P	1939	Bass
Doc Bass	PH	1918	Bass
Kevin Bass	OF	1982-1995	Bass

Player Name	Position	Years Played	Animal
Norm Bass	P	1961-1963	Bass
Randy Bass	1B	1977-1982	Bass
Charley Bassett	3B	1884-1892	Bass
Johnny Bassler	C	1913-1927	Bass
Emil Batch	3B	1904-1907	Bat
Rafael Batista	1B	1973-1975	Bat
Tony Batista	3B	1996-2007	Bat
Miguel Batista	P	1996-2012	Bat
Kevin Batiste	OF	1989	Bat
Kim Batiste	3B	1991-1996	Bat
Larry Battam	3B	1895	Bat
George Batten	2B	1912	Bat
Earl Battey	C	1955-1967	Bat
Joe Battin	3B	1871-1890	Bat
Allen Battle	OF	1995-1999	Bat
Howard Battle	3B	1995-2001	Bat
Jim Battle	3B	1927	Bat
Chris Batton	P	1976	Bat
Matt Batts	C	1947-1956	Bat
Doug Bird	P	1973-1983	Bird
Frank Bird	C	1892	Bird
Red Bird	P	1921	Bird
Dave Birdsall	OF	1871-1873	Bird
Harry Byrd	P	1950-1957	Bird
Jeff Byrd	P	1977	Bird
Jim Byrd	PR	1993	Bird
Paul Byrd	P	1995-2009	Bird
Sammy Byrd	OF	1929-1936	Bird

Player Name	Position	Years Played	Animal
Tim Byrdak	P	Current	Bird
Doug Bair	P	1976-1990	Bear
Danny Tartabull	OF	1984-1997	Bull
Jose Tartabull	OF	1962-1970	Bull
Hank Camelli	C	1943-1947	Camel
Tom Metcalf	P	1963	Calf
Travis Metcalf	3B	2007-2009	Calf
Mike Metcalfe	SS	1998-2000	Calf
Jose Cardenal	CF	1963-1980	Cardinal
Frank Catalanotto	1B	1997-2009	Cat
Tom Catterson	OF	1908-1909	Cat
Ray Katt	C	1952-1959	Cat
Bob Katz	P	1944	Cat
Travis Chick	P	2006-2008	Chick
Lou Collier	LF	1997-2004	Collie
Orlin Collier	P	1931	Collie
Billy Cowan	CF	1963-1972	Cow
Al Cowens	RF	1974-1986	Cow
Colin Cowgill	OF	Current	Cow
Joe Cowley	P	1982-1987	Cow
Roy Crabb	P	1912	Crab
Callix Crabbe	2B	2007-2008	Crab
Estel Crabtree	OF	1929-1944	Crab
Tim Crabtree	P	1995-2001	Crab
Ed Crane	P	1884-1893	Crane
Sam Crane	2B	1880-1890	Crane
Sam Crane	SS	1914-1922	Crane
Ed Kranepool	1B	1962-1979	Crane

Player Name	Position	Years Played	Animal
Rob Deer	RF	1984-1996	Deer
John Deering	P	1903	Deer
Jim Duckworth	P	1963-1966	Duck
Brandon Duckworth	P	Current	Duck
Harry Eells	P	1906	Eel
Pete Falcone	P	1975-1984	Falcon
Joel Finch	P	1979	Finch
Bill Fincher	P	1916	Finch
Sam Fishburn	1B	1919	Fish
John Fishel	OF	1988	Fish
Leo Fishel	P	1899	Fish
Bob Fisher	2B	1912-1919	Fish/Fisher
Brian Fisher	P	1985-1992	Fish/Fisher
Carolos Fisher	P	Current	Fish/Fisher
Chauncey Fisher	P	1893-1901	Fish/Fisher
Cherokee Fisher	3B	1871-1878	Fish/Fisher
Clarence Fisher	P	1919-1920	Fish/Fisher
Don Fisher	P	1945	Fish/Fisher
Ed Fisher	P	1902	Fish/Fisher
Eddie Fisher	P	1959-1973	Fish/Fisher
Fritz Fisher	P	1964	Fish/Fisher
Gus Fisher	C	1911-1912	Fish/Fisher
Harry Fisher	P	1951-1952	Fish/Fisher
Jack Fisher	P	1959-1969	Fish/Fisher
Maurice Fisher	P	1955	Fish/Fisher
Newt Fisher	C	1898	Fish/Fisher
Ray Fisher	P	1910-1920	Fish/Fisher
Red Fisher	OF	1910	Fish/Fisher

Player Name	Position	Years Played	Animal
Showboat Fisher	OF	1923-1932	Fish/Fisher
Tom Fisher	P	1904	Fish/Fisher
Tom Fisher	P	1967	Fish/Fisher
Wilbur Fisher	PH	1916	Fish/Fisher
Stu Flythe	P	1936	Fly
Bob Garbark	C	1934-1945	Gar
Mike Garbark	C	1944-1945	Gar
Bob Garber	P	1956	Gar
Gene Garber	P	1969-1988	Gar
Barbaro Garbey	OF	1984-1988	Gar
Alex Garbowski	PR	1952	Gar
Rich Garces	P	1990-2005	Gar
Amaury Garcia	3B	1999-2000	Gar
Anderson Garcia	P	2007-2008	Gar
Carlos Garcia	2B	1990-1999	Gar
Chico Garcia	2B	1954	Gar
Damaso Garcia	2B	1978-1989	Gar
Danny Garcia	OF	1981	Gar
Danny Garcia	2B	2003-2004	Gar
Freddy Garcia	3B	1995-2000	Gar
Guillermo Garcia	C	1998-1999	Gar
Jesse Garcia	2B	1999-2008	Gar
Jose Garcia	P	2006-2007	Gar
Kiko Garcia	SS	1976-1985	Gar
Leo Garcia	OF	1987-1988	Gar
Luis Garcia	SS	1999	Gar
Luis C. Garcia	RF	2002	Gar
Miguel Garcia	P	1987-1989	Gar

Player Name	Position	Years Played	Animal
Mike Garcia	P	1999-2000	Gar
Mike Garcia	P	1948-1961	Gar
Pedro Garcia	2B	1973-1977	Gar
Ralph Garcia	P	1972-1974	Gar
Ramon Garcia	P	1948	Gar
Ramon Garcia	P	1991-1997	Gar
Reynaldo Garcia	P	2002-2003	Gar
Rosman Garcia	P	2003-2004	Gar
Nomar Garciaparra	1B	1996-2009	Gar
Al Gardella	1B	1945	Gar
Danny Gardella	PH	1944-1950	Gar
Ron Gardenhire	SS	1981-1985	Gar
Art Gardiner	P	1923	Gar
Mike Gardiner	P	1990-1995	Gar
Art Gardner	PH	1975-1978	Gar
Billy Gardner	2B	1954-1963	Gar
Chris Gardner	P	1991	Gar
Earle Gardner	2B	1908-1912	Gar
Gid Gardner	2B	1879-1888	Gar
Glenn Gardner	P	1945	Gar
Harry Gardner	P	1911-1912	Gar
Jeff Gardner	3B	1991-1994	Gar
Jim Gardner	P	1895-1902	Gar
Larry Gardner	3B	1908-1924	Gar
Lee Gardner	P	2002-2008	Gar
Mark Gardner	P	1989-2001	Gar
Ray Gardner	SS	1929-1930	Gar
Rob Gardner	P	1965-1973	Gar

Player Name	Position	Years Played	Animal
Wes Gardner	P	1984-1991	Gar
Bill Garfield	P	1889-1890	Gar
Art Garibaldi	3B	1936	Gar
Bob Garibaldi	P	1962-1969	Gar
Daniel Garibay	P	2000	Gar
Lou Garland	P	1931	Gar
Wayne Garland	P	1973-1981	Gar
Mike Garman	P	1969-1978	Gar
Debs Garms	OF	1932-1945	Gar
Phil Garner	3B	1973-1988	Gar
Willie Garoni	P	1899	Gar
Ralph Garr	DH	1968-1980	Gar
Scott Garrelts	P	1982-1991	Gar
Ned Garver	P	1948-1961	Gar
Steve Garvey	1B	1969-1987	Gar
Jerry Garvin	P	1977-1982	Gar
Victor Garate	P	Current	Gar
Avisail Garcia	RF	Current	Gar
Christian Garcia	P	Current	Gar
Freddy Garcia	P	Current	Gar
Greg Garcia	SS	Current	Gar
Harvey Garcia	P	Current	Gar
Jaime Garcia	P	Current	Gar
Karim Garcia	RF	Current	Gar
Leury Garcia	2B	Current	Gar
Luis Garcia	P	Current	Gar
Onelki Garcia	P	Current	Gar
Yimi Garcia	P	Current	Gar

Player Name	Position	Years Played	Animal
Brett Gardner	CF	Current	Gar
Ryan Garko	1B	Current	Gar
Jon Garland	P	Current	Gar
Cole Garner	LF	Current	Gar
Matt Garza	P	Current	Gar
Shawn Hare	OF	1991-1995	Hare
Jerry Hairston	OF	1973-1989	Hare
Johnny Hairston	OF	1969	Hare
Sammy Hairston	C	1951	Hare
Jerry Hairston	3B	Current	Hare
Scott Hairston	OF	Current	Hare
Ed Hawk	P	1911	Hawk
Bill Hawke	P	1892-1894	Hawk
Andy Hawkins	P	1982-1991	Hawk
Wynn Hawkins	P	1960-1962	Hawk
Chicken Hawks	1B	1921-1925	Hawk
LaTroy Hawkins	P	Current	Hawk
Blake Hawksworth	P	Current	Hawk
Bert Hogg	3B	1934	Hog
Bill Hogg	P	1905-1908	Hog
Brad Hogg	P	1911-1919	Hog
Chief Yellowhorse	P	1921-1922	Horse
Hanson Horsey	P	1912	Horse
Butch Huskey	RF	1993-2001	Huskey
Jake Jaeckel	P	1964	Jackal
David Lamb	3B	1999-2002	Lamb
John Lamb	P	1970-1973	Lamb
Lyman Lamb	3B	1920-1921	Lamb

Player Name	Position	Years Played	Animal
Mike Lamb	1B	2000-2009	Lamb
Ray Lamb	P	1969-1973	Lamb
Freddy Leach	OF	1923-1932	Leach
Jalal Leach	RF	2001	Leach
Rick Leach	OF	1981-1990	Leach
Terry Leach	P	1981-1993	Leach
Tommy Leach	OF	1898-1918	Leach
Brent Leach	P	Current	Leach
Fenton Mole	1B	1949	Mole
Bob Moose	P	1967-1976	Moose
Mike Mussina	P	1991-2008	Moose
Doc Newton	P	1900-1909	Newt
Luis Olmo	OF	1943-1951	Olm
Fred Olmstead	P	1908-1911	Olm
Al Olmsted	P	1980	Olm
Hank Olmsted	P	1905	Olm
Ray Olmedo	SS	Current	Olm
Edgar Olmos	P	Current	Olm
Billy Otterson	SS	1887	Otter
Jim Panther	P	1971-1973	Panther
Jiggs Parrott	3B	1892-1895	Parrott
Mike Parrott	P	1977-1981	Parrott
Tom Parrott	OF	1893-1896	Parrott
Johnny Peacock	C	1937-1945	Peacock
Brad Peacock	P	Current	Peacock
Joe Pignatano	C	1957-1962	Pig
Carmen Pignatiello	P	2007-2008	Pig
Jess Pike	OF	1946	Pike

Player Name	Position	Years Played	Animal
Joe Rabbitt	OF	1922	Rabbitt
Gene Ratliff	PH	1965	Rat
Jon Ratliff	P	1999-2000	Rat
Paul Ratliff	C	1963-1972	Rat
Steve Ratzer	P	1980-1981	Rat
Jason Roach	P	2003	Roach
John Roach	P	1887	Roach
Mel Roach	3B	1953-1962	Roach
Roxey Roach	SS	1910-1915	Roach
Skel Roach	P	1899	Roach
Brad Salmon	P	2007-2008	Salmon
Chico Salmon	SS	1964-1972	Salmon
Roger Salmon	P	1912	Salmon
Tim Salmon	DH	1992-2006	Salmon
Bert Shepard	P	1945	Shepherd
Jack Shepard	C	1953-1956	Shepherd
Ray Shepardson	C	1924	Shepherd
Keith Shepherd	P	1992-1996	Shepherd
Ron Shepherd	OF	1984-1986	Shepherd
Alan Storke	SS	1906-1909	Stork
Craig Swan	P	1973-1984	Swan
Russ Swan	P	1989-1994	Swan
Pinky Swander	OF	1903-1904	Swan
Pedro Swann	RF	2000-2007	Swan
Bill Swanson	2B	1914	Swan
Evar Swanson	OF	1929-1934	Swan
Karl Swanson	2B	1928-1929	Swan
Red Swanson	P	1955-1957	Swan

Player Name	Position	Years Played	Animal
Stan Swanson	OF	1971	Swan
Dizzy Trout	P	1939-1957	Trout
Steve Trout	P	1978-1989	Trout
Mike Trout	OF	Current	Trout
Ernie Wolf	P	1912	Wolf
Jimmy Wolf	OF	1882-1892	Wolf
Lefty Wolf	P	1921	Wolf
Ray Wolf	1B	1927	Wolf

The Final Team

The Pitching Staff

Starting Pitcher 1 – Ted Lyons (lion). You can hear the roar of this Hall of Fame pitcher. With 260 career wins and a 3.67 ERA, this animal is king of this team's rotational jungle.

Starting Pitcher 2 – Mike Mussina (moose). With 270 career wins and a 3.68 career ERA, Moose measures favorably to Ted Lyons. The only reason I kept the Moose at #2 is he has yet to be voted into the Hall of Fame.

Starting Pitcher 3 – Dizzy Trout. Lucky for Dizzy that Mike Trout does not have the longevity yet to make the All-Time Animal Team. Dizzy's 170 career wins and 3.25 ERA gave Dizzy the nod over Steve Trout.

Starting Pitcher 4 – Johnny Antonelli (ant). A six-time All-Star for the NY/SF Giants, Johnny was no ant on the mound but makes this team as one. He compiled 126 career wins and a 3.34 ERA. His best season was 1954 for the World Champion Giants, when he led the league in ERA (2.30), batting average against (.219) and shutouts (six). He was the winning starting pitcher in Game 2 of the 1954 World Series and entered Game 4 in relief to thwart a Cleveland rally, leading the Giants to a World Series sweep.

Starting Pitcher 5 – Eddie Fisher (fisher or fish). Eddie got the nod as the fifth starter for his versatility and his name. While primarily a reliever, Eddie started 63 games and appeared in a total of 690 games. He finished his career with 85 wins and a 3.41 ERA and, more impressively, saved 81 games in 89 chances.

Closer – Gene Garber (gar). Garber got the nod over Doug Bird and Doug Bair. Closer was a tough choice because gar is a common animal name, and I looked at including Ralph Garr on the team. In the end, though, I selected another bird (type) and went with Gene's 218 career saves (39th all-time and first among the animals).

The Outfield
Center Field – Jose Cardenal (cardinal). This named cardinal, who also played for the Cardinals in 1970, makes the team as the center fielder. As previously noted, I looked at Ralph Garr to fill this role but went with Gene Garber at closer instead. Cardenal also earned the spot since his primary position was center field, whereas Ralph was primarily a left fielder. Cardenal amassed 1,913 career hits and a lifetime .275 batting average and .333 on-base percentage.

Right Field – Frank Robinson got the nod over Brooks for top Robin and other lesser animal candidates such as Jimmy Wolf and Rob Deer. Frank's career numbers included a .294 batting average, .389 on-base percentage and 586 home runs.

Left Field – Rickey Henderson. Rounding out the all-bird outfield, this Hen was the easiest selection to make. Rickey compiled 3,055 hits in his career, go along with 1,406 stolen bases. His lifetime .401 on-base percentage puts him in the top 60 of all-time.

The Infield & Designated Hitter

Catcher – Mickey Cochrane. Mickey got the nod over Earl Battey. While Earl had a very respectable career spanning 1955 to 1967, he was not a Hall of Famer. Mickey finished his Hall of Fame career with a .320 batting average and .419 on-base percentage, numbers certainly not for the birds.

First Base – Jimmie Fox. Jimmie got the nod over fellow Hall of Famer Nellie Fox. While position played a role, Jimmie was one of the greatest first basemen ever to play the game. He finished his career (1925 – 1945) with 534 home runs and 2,646 hits. Jimmie combined power and plate discipline, finishing with a .325 batting average and .428 on-base percentage. His best year was 1932, when he had a .364 batting average, hit 58 home runs and drove in 169 runs. Incredibly, Jimmie finished second in batting that season, and it wasn't until the following year that he won the triple crown with a .356 batting average, 48 home runs and 163 RBIs.

Second Base – Joe Morgan. Joe got the nod over fellow Hall of Famers Nellie Fox and Jackie Robinson. Lucky for me that this "horse" was available. Joe is considered one of the best second basemen of all time. In his 21-year career (1963 – 1984), Joe had 2,517 hits, 689 stolen bases, 268 home runs, a .271 batting average and a .392 on-base percentage. His longevity also factored into the decision.

Shortstop – Barry Larkin. This was an easy choice, as Barry is a Hall of Fame shortstop who finished his career with 2,340 hits, a .295 batting average and a .371 on-base percentage.

Third Base – Tommy Leach. With 2,143 career hits (1898 – 1918), a .269 batting average and a .340 on-base percentage, Tommy made the team in what amounted to trickle-down economics. Selecting Gene Garber as closer eliminated Larry Gardner, and selecting Frank Robinson in right field eliminated Brooks Robinson. A versatile player, Tommy played both third base and center field. Showing how the game has changed, Tommy led the league in 1902 with only six home runs.

DH – Tim Salmon. Tim is all over this book as salmon also is a color and a food. This fish rounded out the team with his .282 batting average and .385 on-base percentage. His 1,674 career hits and 299 home runs are also noteworthy.

Chapter Six
The All-Time
My Last Name is Also a First Name Team

Overview

There are countless Major Leaguers whose last names can easily be confused with first names. Hank Aaron, Frank Robinson and all-time hits leader Pete Rose, for example, are all great players also having the distinction that their last names can be used as first names.

To be included on this team, a player's surname must also be the first name of a person (masculine or feminine).

In the case of masculine names, the name must be one that has been represented in the Major Leagues.

Fun Facts
- More than 20% of players inducted into the Hall of Fame have a surname that can be used a person's first name.
- Of those players, all positions are represented.
- There was one Major Leaguer whose first name was Johnson (Johnson Fry, a pitcher in 1923 for the Cleveland Indians) and one whose first name was Gibson (Gibson Alba, a pitcher for the St. Louis Cardinals in 1988), thus qualifying Walter Johnson and Bob and Josh Gibson as candidates for the team.
- There have been more players with a first name of Robinson (five) than Carlton (three).

- There has been one player with the first name Palmer – Palmer Hildebrand, a catcher in 1913 for the St. Louis Browns.
- Three players have had the first name Winfield but none has had the first name Wilhelm – although there was a Wilhelmus (Remerswaal).

Thought Process on Team Selection

To narrow down the list of candidates, I decided the player must be in the Hall of Fame, with one notable exception made for a player who should be inducted. Sorry Pete Rose, it is not you.

I made no distinction between masculine and feminine names, except in the case of masculine last names, I had to confirm that the name existed as another player's first name.

The Final Team

The Pitching Staff

Starting Pitcher 1 – Walter Johnson. The Big Train heads the rotation, with a career 417-279 record and 2.11 ERA. His 3,508 strikeouts, 1.06 WHIP and 110 shutouts are the stuff of legends.

Starting Pitcher 2 – Bob Gibson. In 1968, Bob Gibson went 22-9 with a 1.12 ERA. He walked only 62 batters and struck out 268 in 304.2 innings. The following year, Major League Baseball reduced the height of the mound. Any pitcher who can literally change the rules of the game is worthy of this team. By the way, Gibson followed up his near-perfect season with a 20 – 13 record and a 2.18 ERA. Lifetime, he owns a 251-174 record and 2.91 ERA.

Starting Pitcher 3 – Steve Carlton. With a 329-244 career record, 3.22 ERA and 4,136 strikeouts, Carlton was one of the dominant left handers of his generation, though often pitching on poor teams. His 1972 season is one of the greatest seasons ever for a pitcher. Carlton went 27 – 10 with a 1.97 ERA. He struck out 310 batters in 346.1 innings. Even more staggering is that Steve won 47% of all games won by the Phillies that year.

Starting Pitcher 4 – Grover Alexander. A career record of 373-208, 2.56 ERA and 90 shutouts made Grover an easy choice for the rotation.

Starting Pitcher 5 – Satchel Paige. While he may have an effeminate surname, on the mound he was all man. Paige is considered by most baseball historians as the greatest pitcher in Negro League history and one of the greatest ever to play the game. When he was finally able to compete in the Major Leagues starting in 1948, at the age of 42, he still managed to win 28 games, with four shutouts and a 3.29 ERA, which left people wondering what might have been had he been allowed to compete in his prime.

Closer – Nolan Ryan. Ryan began his career as a relief pitcher and actually has three saves on his resume, to go along with his 324-292 record, 3.19 ERA and 5,714 career strikeouts in 5,386 innings. Since there is no mistaking the surnames of fellow Hall of Famers Fingers and Gossage for first names, we went with the Ryan Express as our closer. It is often said that relievers gain a few extra miles per hour on their fastball, so it is a scary thought to think what Ryan could have done as a modern-day closer.

The Outfield

Right Field – Babe Ruth. The most first-name-heavy member of this team had to be the Sultan of Swat himself, George Herman Ruth (Babe). While probably no one ever mistook the Babe for a Ruth, he decidedly met the criteria to be included on this theme team. His .342 lifetime batting average and .474 lifetime on-base percentage are ninth and second all-time, respectively.

Center Field – Hack Wilson. Lewis "Hack" Wilson got the nod over fellow Hall of Famer Max Carey. More recent candidates like Fred Lynn, Al Oliver, Amos Otis and Dale Murphy stack up well, but Hack's lifetime .307 batting average and .395 on-base percentage are a welcome addition to any team. Wilson may not be the most common first name but it is shared by current Major Leaguers such as Wilson Alvarez, Wilson Betemit and Wilson Valdez.

Left Field – Joe Jackson. Jackson is the one member of this team who is not in the Hall of Fame, but he did get the nod over Rickey Henderson. Jackson had a lifetime .356 batting average, which ranks him third all-time. The Hall of Fame might not put Joe on their team, but he is the best left fielder whose last name is also a first name. Interestingly enough, only one Major League player had the first name Jackson. Pitcher Jackson Todd played for the Mets and Blue Jays.

The Infield and Designated Hitter

Catcher – Gary Carter. The selection of Bob Gibson as pitcher eliminated Josh Gibson from consideration. As such, I went with The Kid, who also has the distinction of being on the All-Time Presidents Team and Occupation Team.

First Base – Eddie Murray. Eddie was one of the most feared hitters of his generation. A switch hitter, Murray amassed 3,255 hits over his career spanning 1977 – 1997. Add to his resume 504 home runs, a .287 batting average and a .359 on-base percentage, and it is easy to see why Murray is in the Hall of Fame.

Second Base – Jackie Robinson. I went with Jackie over Joe Morgan. Robinson finished his career with a .311 batting average .409 on-base percentage. He was successful on 86% of his stolen base attempts and often caused nightmares for pitchers on the base paths.

Third Base – George Brett. Brett gets the nod over Mike Schmidt, as no players have had the first name Schmidt. Brett's career totals of 3,154 hits, a .305 batting average, a .369 on-base percentage and 317 home runs made him an easy choice for this team.

Shortstop – Joseph "Arky" Vaughan. He got the nod over fellow Hall of Famers John Ward, Bobby Wallace, Pee Wee Reese, Pop Lloyd, Travis Jackson and George Davis. Vaughan's lifetime .308 batting average and .406 on-base percentage made him a worthy member of this team.

DH – Hank Aaron. Aaron ranks at the top of most career offensive statistical categories, so I could not leave him off this team. He finished his career with 3,771 hits (third-most in history), 755 home runs (second), 2,174 runs scored (fourth) and 2,297 RBI's (first). His .305 batting average and .375 on-base percentage, while not in the top 10, certainly also contribute to his status as one of the greatest ever to play the game.

Chapter Seven
The All-Time Flora Team

Overview

A (Pete) Rose by any other name would still smell as sweet and would still not be in the Hall of Fame. That is why we plant our (Bob) Seeds so that they grow a strong (Charley) Root system and blossom into a (Donie) Bush, all while making sure the (Norm) Branch of our soaring (Howard) Maple and (Ken) Ash trees that were (Erik) Planten(berg) in our (Lefty) Grove are not covered with (Mike) Ivie or (Bob) Vines. While we certainly want our (Dave) Vineyard to yield plenty of (Bobby) Wine, this team will serve no wine (whether or not before its time). To be considered for this theme team, I was looking for player surnames containing trees, plants, flowers or parts of any of them (*e.g.*, branches, petals and roots). Other flora-related words, such as grove, plant, woods and seed, also qualify, but Garden, Bur and Wood do not.

The full list of the 134 flora terms used in selecting this team is as follows (terms in **bold** indicate Major League representation):

Alder	Carnation	**Fir**	Lilac	**Rose**
Amaranth	Catalpa	**Flora**	**Lily**	Rosemary
Amaryllis	Cedar	**Flower**	Locust	**Sage**
Anemone	**Cherry**	**Forest**	Lotus	**Seed**
Apple	Chestnut	Foxglove	Madrone	Shrub
Ash	**Chiles**	Freesia	**Maple**	Snapdragon
Aspen	Chinquapins	Gerbera	Marigold	**Sprout**
Aster	Chrysanthemum	Gladiolus	Marjoram	Spruce

Azalea	Clover	**Grass**	Mimosa	**Stem**
Bark	**Cole**	**Grove**	**Moss**	Sunflower
Basswood	Columbine	**Hay**	**Nettle**	Sycamore
Beech	Cottonwood	**Hazel**	Narcissus	Tansy
Begonia	**Cress**	Heather	**Oak**	Thistle
Bellflower	Crocus	**Hedge**	Orchid	Thyme
Bergamot	Cypress	Hemlock	**Pear**	**Tree**
Birch	Daffodil	**Hemp**	Peony	Tulip
Bloom	Dahlia	Hibiscus	Petunia	**Vine**
Blossom	**Daisy**	**Holly**	Pine	**Vineyard**
Bluebell	Delphinium	Hyacinth	**Pit**	Violet
Bouquet	**Dill**	Iris	**Plant**	Walnut
Bottlebrush	Dogwood	**Ivy**	Poplar	**Weed**
Branch	Edelweiss	Jasmine	**Posey**	**Wheat**
Buckeye	**Elm**	Juniper	Primrose	**Woods**
Bud	**Fennel**	Larch	Redwood	Willow
Bush	**Fern**	Lavender	**Reed**	**Yew**
Buttercup	**Fig**	**Leaf**	Rhododendron	Zinnia
Camellias	Filbert	**Lemon**	**Root**	

<u>Fun Facts</u>
- The Hall of Fame has a grove in Robert "Lefty" Grove, an ash tree in Richie Ashburn, a lemon tree in Bob Lemon and wheat grain in Zach Wheat. It also features executive Cumberland "pocket full of" Posey, and if first names counted, it would also have executive Branch Rickey.

- Of the 134 flora terms listed above, fewer than half (62) have been represented in Major League Baseball.
- Rose is by far the most popular flora name. There have been seven Roses, in addition to 29 other players with "Rose" as part of their surnames, including notables such as Al Rosen.
- Reed is the next most-common flora name, followed by Dill, Bush and Bark.
- Besides two players with the last name Grove, there has been a Cosgrove, Hargrove and Hardgrove.
- Charlie Furbush can be counted as a fir tree or a bush.
- Zach Wheat has the highest flora career batting average, at .317. No wonder he is in the Hall of Fame.
- Lefty Grove is the all-time flora career wins leader, with 300.
- Notable terms not used in selecting the team: bur, collard, cork, garden, glade, pip, sod, testa, wilts, wither, wood.
- The complete list of flora players derived from the list of 134 terms shown above includes:

Flora Player	Position	Years Active	Flora Term
Dale Alderson	P	1943-1944	Alder
Fred Applegate	P	1904-1904	Apple
Ed Appleton	P	1915-1916	Apple
Pete Appleton	P	1927-1945	Apple
Ed Wineapple	P	1929-1929	Apple
Cody Asche	LF	2013-2015	Ash
Ken Ash	P	1925-1930	Ash
Richie Ashburn	OF	1948-1962	Ash

Flora Player	Position	Years Active	Flora Term
Alan Ashby	C	1973-1989	Ash
Andy Ashby	P	1991-2004	Ash
Tucker Ashford	3B	1976-1984	Ash
Billy Ashley	LF	1992-1998	Ash
Nevin Ashley	C	2015-2015	Ash
Brian Bark	P	1995-1995	Bark
Al Barker	LF	1871-1871	Bark
Glen Barker	CF	1999-2001	Bark
Kevin Barker	1B	1999-2009	Bark
Len Barker	P	1976-1987	Bark
Ray Barker	1B	1960-1967	Bark
Richie Barker	P	1999-1999	Bark
Sean Barker	LF	2007-2007	Bark
Andy Barkett	1B	2001-2001	Bark
Brian Barkley	P	1998-1998	Bark
Jeff Barkley	P	1984-1985	Bark
Red Barkley	2B	1937-1943	Bark
Sam Barkley	2B	1884-1889	Bark
Mike Garbark	C	1944-1945	Bark
Bob Garbark	C	1934-1945	Bark
Matt Beech	P	1996-1998	Beech
Ed Beecher	LF	1887-1891	Beech
Roy Beecher	P	1907-1908	Beech
Al Burch	CF	1906-1911	Birch
Ernie Burch	LF	1884-1887	Birch
Bud Bloomfield	2B	1963-1964	Bloom
Willie	SS	2002-2015	Bloom

Flora Player	Position	Years Active	Flora Term
Bloomquist			
Red Bluhm	PH	1918-1918	Bloom
Clint Blume	P	1922-1923	Bloom
Bill Monbouquette	P	1958-1968	Bouquet
Harvey Branch	P	1962-1962	Branch
Norm Branch	P	1941-1942	Branch
Roy Branch	P	1979-1979	Branch
Garland Buckeye	P	1918-1928	Buckeye
Jay Budd	LF	1890-1890	Bud
Ed Busch	SS	1943-1945	Bush
Mike Busch	3B	1995-1996	Bush
Brian Buscher	3B	2007-2009	Bush
Don Buschhorn	P	1965-1965	Bush
Dave Bush	P	2004-2013	Bush
Guy Bush	P	1923-1945	Bush
Homer Bush	2B	1997-2004	Bush
Bullet Joe Bush	P	1912-1928	Bush
Donie Bush	SS	1908-1923	Bush
Randy Bush	OF	1982-1993	Bush
Jack Bushelman	P	1909-1912	Bush
Frank Bushey	P	1927-1930	Bush
Chris Bushing	P	1993-1993	Bush
Doc Bushong	C	1875-1890	Bush
Kevin Quackenbush	P	2014-2015	Bush
Rocky Cherry	P	2007-2008	Cherry
Pearce Chiles	1B	1899-1900	Chiles
Rich Chiles	LF	1971-1978	Chiles
Bert Cole	P	1921-1927	Cole
Alex Cole	CF	1990-1996	Cole

Flora Player	Position	Years Active	Flora Term
A. J. Cole	P	2015-2015	Cole
Dave Cole	P	1950-1955	Cole
Ed Cole	P	1938-1939	Cole
Gerrit Cole	P	2013-2015	Cole
King Cole	P	1909-1915	Cole
Dick Cole	SS	1951-1957	Cole
Stu Cole	2B	1991-1991	Cole
Victor Cole	P	1992-1992	Cole
Willis Cole	CF	1909-1910	Cole
Walker Cress	P	1948-1949	Cress
Jack Cressend	P	2000-2004	Cress
George Daisy	P	1884-1884	Daisy
Bill Caudill	P	1979-1987	Dill
Don Dillard	LF	1959-1965	Dill
Gordon Dillard	P	1988-1989	Dill
Pat Dillard	3B	1900-1900	Dill
Steve Dillard	2B	1975-1982	Dill
Tim Dillard	P	2008-2012	Dill
Pickles Dillhoefer	C	1917-1921	Dill
Harley Dillinger	P	1914-1914	Dill
Bob Dillinger	3B	1946-1951	Dill
Bill Dillman	P	1967-1970	Dill
Pop Dillon	1B	1899-1904	Dill
John Dillon	SS	1875-1875	Dill
Joe Dillon	2B	2005-2009	Dill
Packy Dillon	C	1875-1875	Dill
Steve Dillon	P	1963-1964	Dill
Miguel Dilone	LF	1974-1985	Dill
Jake Elmore	2B	2012-2015	Elm
Verdo Elmore	RF	1924-1924	Elm

Flora Player	Position	Years Active	Flora Term
Frank Fennelly	SS	1884-1890	Fennel
Ed Fernandes	C	1940-1946	Fern
Alex Fernandez	P	1990-2000	Fern
Sid Fernandez	P	1983-1997	Fern
Frank Fernandez	C	1967-1972	Fern
Nanny Fernandez	3B	1942-1950	Fern
Chico Fernandez	SS	1956-1963	Fern
Jared Fernandez	P	2001-2006	Fern
Jose Fernandez	P	2013-2015	Fern
Jose Fernandez	3B	1999-2001	Fern
Chico Fernandez	SS	1968-1968	Fern
Tony Fernandez	SS	1983-2001	Fern
Osvaldo Fernandez	P	1996-2001	Fern
Buck Redfern	2B	1928-1929	Fern
Pete Redfern	P	1976-1982	Fern
Alfredo Figaro	P	2009-2014	Fig
Mike Figga	C	1997-1999	Fig
Frank Figgemeier	P	1894-1894	Fig
Chone Figgins	P	2002-2014	Fig
Bien Figueroa	SS	1992-1992	Fig
Ed Figueroa	P	1974-1981	Fig
Jesus Figueroa	CF	1980-1980	Fig
Luis Figueroa	SS	2001-2007	Fig
Nelson Figueroa	P	2000-2011	Fig
Pedro Figueroa	P	2012-2014	Fig
Cole Figueroa	2B	2014-2015	Fig
Dan Firova	C	1981-1988	Fir

Flora Player	Position	Years Active	Flora Term
John Firth	P	1884-1884	Fir
Rafael Furcal	SS	2000-2014	Fir
Carl Furillo	RF	1946-1960	Fir
J. J. Furmaniak	SS	2005-2007	Fir
Charlie Furbush	P	2011-2015	Fir, Bush
Kevin Flora	CF	1991-1995	Flora
Harry Colliflower	P	1899-1899	Flower
Ben Flowers	P	1951-1956	Flower
Dickie Flowers	SS	1871-1872	Flower
Wes Flowers	P	1940-1944	Flower
Tyler Flowers	C	2009-2015	Flower
Jake Flowers	2B	1923-1934	Flower
Ty LaForest	3B	1945-1945	Forest
Pete LaForest	C	2003-2007	Forest
Jim Greengrass	LF	1952-1956	Grass
Ed Pipgras	P	1932-1932	Grass
George Pipgras	P	1923-1935	Grass
Chappie Snodgrass	OF	1901-1901	Grass
Mike Cosgrove	P	1972-1976	Grove
Orval Grove	P	1940-1949	Grove
Lefty Grove	P	1925-1941	Grove
Charley Grover	P	1913-1913	Grove
Roy Grover	2B	1916-1919	Grove
Pat Hardgrove	PH	1918-1918	Grove
Mike Hargrove	1B	1974-1985	Grove
Ed Haigh	RF	1892-1892	Hay
Dirk Hayhurst	P	2008-2009	Hay
Fred Hayner	P	1890-1890	Hay
Red Hayworth	C	1944-1945	Hay
Ray Hayworth	C	1926-1945	Hay

Flora Player	Position	Years Active	Flora Term
Doc Hazelton	1B	1902-1902	Hazel
Bob Hazle	RF	1955-1958	Hazel
Austin Hedges	C	2015-2015	Hedge
Harry Hedgpeth	P	1913-1913	Hedge
Ducky Hemp	CF	1887-1890	Hemp
Bret Hemphill	C	1999-1999	Hemp
Charlie Hemphill	CF	1899-1911	Hemp
Frank Hemphill	LF	1906-1909	Hemp
Ed Holley	P	1928-1934	Holly
Ed Holly	SS	1906-1915	Holly
Jeff Holly	P	1977-1979	Holly
Mike Ivie	1B	1971-1983	Ivy
Jimmy Lavender	P	1912-1917	Lavender
Jeff Liefer	1B	1999-2005	Leaf
Chet Lemon	OF	1975-1990	Lemon
Jim Lemon	RF	1950-1963	Lemon
Bob Lemon	P	1941-1958	Lemon
Dave Lemonds	P	1969-1972	Lemon
Mark Lemongello	P	1976-1979	Lemon
Brent Lillibridge	2B	2008-2013	Lilly
Jim Lillie	OF	1883-1886	Lilly
Ted Lilly	P	1999-2013	Lilly
Rolla Mapel	P	1919-1919	Maple
Howard Maple	C	1932-1932	Maple
Brandon Moss	LF	2007-2015	Moss
Charlie Moss	C	1934-1936	Moss
Mal Moss	P	1930-1930	Moss
Damian Moss	P	2001-2004	Moss
Howie Moss	3B	1942-1946	Moss
Les Moss	C	1946-1958	Moss

Flora Player	Position	Years Active	Flora Term
Ray Moss	P	1926-1931	Moss
Graig Nettles	3B	1967-1988	Nettle
Jim Nettles	CF	1970-1981	Nettle
Morris Nettles	CF	1974-1975	Nettle
Rebel Oakes	CF	1909-1915	Oak
Frank Pears	P	1889-1893	Pear
Albie Pearson	CF	1958-1966	Pear
Alex Pearson	P	1902-1903	Pear
Ike Pearson	P	1939-1948	Pear
Jason Pearson	P	2002-2003	Pear
Monte Pearson	P	1932-1941	Pear
Terry Pearson	P	2002-2002	Pear
Pete LePine	RF	1902-1902	Pine
Jake Pitler	2B	1917-1918	Pit
Skip Pitlock	P	1970-1975	Pit
Chris Pittaro	3B	1985-1987	Pit
Pinky Pittenger	SS	1921-1929	Pit
Togie Pittinger	P	1900-1907	Pit
Joe Pittman	2B	1981-1984	Pit
Gaylen Pitts	3B	1974-1975	Pit
Jim Pittsley	P	1995-1999	Pit
Stan Pitula	P	1957-1957	Pit
Herman Pitz	C	1890-1890	Pit
Erik Plantenberg	P	1993-1997	Plant
Phil Plantier	OF	1990-1997	Plant
Cum Posey	Executive	-	Posey
Buster Posey	C	2009-2015	Posey
Addison Reed	P	2011-2015	Reed
Chris Reed	P	2015-2015	Reed
Darren Reed	RF	1990-1992	Reed
Eric Reed	CF	2006-2007	Reed

Flora Player	Position	Years Active	Flora Term
Evan Reed	P	2013-2014	Reed
Howie Reed	P	1958-1971	Reed
Jeff Reed	C	1984-2000	Reed
Jeremy Reed	CF	2004-2011	Reed
Jerry Reed	P	1981-1990	Reed
Jody Reed	2B	1987-1997	Reed
Jack Reed	CF	1961-1963	Reed
Keith Reed	OF	2005-2005	Reed
Michael Reed	CF	2015-2015	Reed
Milt Reed	SS	1911-1915	Reed
Ted Reed	3B	1915-1915	Reed
Rick Reed	P	1988-2003	Reed
Bob Reed	P	1969-1970	Reed
Ron Reed	P	1966-1984	Reed
Steve Reed	P	1992-2005	Reed
Billy Reed	2B	1952-1952	Reed
Earl Reid	P	1946-1946	Reed
Hugh Reid	OF	1874-1874	Reed
Jessie Reid	RF	1987-1988	Reed
Ryan Reid	P	2013-2013	Reed
Scott Reid	CF	1969-1970	Reed
Billy Reid	2B	1883-1884	Reed
Bill Reidy	P	1896-1904	Reed
Charlie Root	P	1923-1941	Root
Dane De La Rosa	P	2011-2014	Rose
Eury De La Rosa	P	2013-2014	Rose
Francisco de la Rosa	P	1991-1991	Rose
Jesus de la Rosa	PH	1975-1975	Rose
Jorge De La Rosa	P	2004-2015	Rose
Rubby De La	P	2011-2015	Rose

Flora Player	Position	Years Active	Flora Term
Rosa			
Tomas de la Rosa	SS	2000-2006	Rose
John LaRose	P	1978-1978	Rose
Vic LaRose	SS	1968-1968	Rose
Mike Roesler	P	1989-1990	Rose
Brian Rose	P	1997-2001	Rose
Chuck Rose	P	1909-1909	Rose
Don Rose	P	1971-1974	Rose
Mike Rose	C	2004-2006	Rose
Pete Rose	3B	1963-1986	Rose
Pete Rose	1B	1997-1997	Rose
Bobby Rose	2B	1989-1992	Rose
John Roseboro	C	1957-1970	Rose
Rosie Rosebraugh	P	1898-1899	Rose
Bob Roselli	C	1955-1962	Rose
Dave Rosello	2B	1972-1981	Rose
Chief Roseman	OF	1882-1890	Rose
Al Rosen	3B	1947-1956	Rose
Goody Rosen	OF	1937-1946	Rose
B. J. Rosenberg	P	2012-2014	Rose
Harry Rosenberg	OF	1930-1930	Rose
Lou Rosenberg	2B	1923-1923	Rose
Steve Rosenberg	P	1988-1991	Rose
Max Rosenfeld	OF	1931-1933	Rose
Larry Rosenthal	OF	1936-1945	Rose
Sy Rosenthal	OF	1925-1926	Rose
Trevor Rosenthal	P	2012-2015	Rose

Flora Player	Position	Years Active	Flora Term
Wayne Rosenthal	P	1991-1992	Rose
Steve Roser	P	1944-1946	Rose
Bunny Roser	OF	1922-1922	Rose
Dave Rozema	P	1977-1986	Rose
Harry Sage	C	1890-1890	Sage
A. J. Sager	P	1994-1998	Sage
Pony Sager	SS	1871-1871	Sage
Bob Seeds	OF	1930-1940	Seed
Bob Sprout	P	1961-1961	Sprout
Fred Stem	1B	1908-1909	Stem
Estel Crabtree	CF	1929-1944	Tree
Tim Crabtree	P	1995-2001	Tree
Nick Tremark	RF	1934-1936	Tree
Joey Devine	P	2005-2011	Vine
Adrian Devine	P	1973-1980	Vine
Mickey Devine	C	1918-1925	Vine
Hal Deviney	P	1920-1920	Vine
Bob Vines	P	1924-1925	Vine
Dave Vineyard	P	1964-1964	Vineyard
Bert Weeden	PH	1911-1911	Weed
Lee Wheat	P	1954-1955	Wheat
Mack Wheat	C	1915-1921	Wheat
Zack Wheat	LF	1909-1927	Wheat
Charlie Wheatley	P	1912-1912	Wheat
Woody Wheaton	OF	1943-1944	Wheat
Al Woods	OF	1977-1986	Woods
Clarence Woods	P	1914-1914	Woods
Gary Woods	CF	1976-1985	Woods
Pinky Woods	P	1943-1945	Woods

Flora Player	Position	Years Active	Flora Term
Jake Woods	P	2005-2008	Woods
Jim Woods	3B	1957-1961	Woods
John Woods	P	1924-1924	Woods
Ron Woods	CF	1969-1974	Woods
Walt Woods	P	1898-1900	Woods
Tom Yewcic	C	1957-1957	Yew
Ed Yewell	2B	1884-1884	Yew

Thought Process on Team Selection

With a total pool of around 300 players and 62 unique terms, filling out a full team seemed achievable. Hall of Famers Lefty Grove (starting pitcher), Bob Lemon (starting pitcher), Zach Wheat (left field) and Richie Ashburn (center field) were locks. Pete Rose's flexibility of playing so many different positions also made him a good fit, subject only to figuring out at which position to use him. After I'd assigned a Wheat, Rose, Grove, Lemon and Ash(burn) and eliminated center fielders and left fielders, the pool of players dropped to around 215, from which emerged the challenge of filling out the remainder of the team.

The Final Team

The Pitching Staff

Starting Pitcher 1 – Robert "Lefty" Grove. This orchard, or small group of trees, stands out as the staff leader on the All-Time Flora Team. Lefty won 300 games against 141 losses, had a career 3.06 ERA and even had 55 saves.

Starting Pitcher 2 – Bob Lemon. This tree bears the fruit of being the Flora Team's number two starter. Lemon won 207 games against 128 losses and had a career 3.23 ERA.

Starting Pitcher 3 – Charlie Root. The foundation of any strong tree is its root system, and this Root makes the team with a cool name and 201 career wins, along with a 3.59 ERA. Charlie Root gained fame by being the pitcher for Babe Ruth's alleged called home run shot during the 1932 World Series.

Starting Pitcher 4 – Sid Fernandez. "El Sid" finished his career with a 114-96 record and a very stingy 3.36 ERA. He made the Flora Team also in large part because of his career 1.14 WHIP. Of course, his inclusion eliminated other Ferns from contention.

Starting Pitcher 5 – Ted Lilly. This lily smells sweet for the Flora Team with his 130 career wins and 4.14 career ERA. Ted pitched his career in the steroid era, so I had to take that into account in his favor. He got the nod over a couple of more deserving "Bush" players, Bullet Joe and Guy, simply because I'd selected a Bush elsewhere.

Honorable Mention
I had to give an honorable mention to Ed Figueroa. In 1978, while pitching for the New York Yankees' World Series champion team, Ed compiled a 20 – 9 record and a 2.99 ERA. Overall in his career, Fig had 80 wins against 67 losses, with an ERA of 3.51.

Closer – Bill Caudill. Dill enhances quite a few food dishes, so this (Cau)dill had to makes this team. His 106 saves didn't hurt, either, so I selected him over cooler-named pitchers such as Norm Branch and Ben Flowers.

The Outfield

Center Field – Richie Ashburn. The best Ash ever to play the game, this Hall of Famer was an easy choice. His 2,574 career hits are more than all the other Ash players' hit totals combined. With his lifetime .308 batting average and .396 on-base percentage, it is easy to see why he is in the Hall of Fame.

Right Field – Bob Seeds. Every plant member of the Flora Team started out as a seed, so it is no wonder that I added Bob Seeds to the team. Bob played all three outfield positions as well as first base, so I liked his versatility as well. In his nine-year career, Bob batted a very respectable .277, with a .336 on-base percentage.

Left Field – Zach Wheat. Hall of Famer Zach Wheat edged out Phil Plantier. Wheat finished his career with 2,884 hits, a .317 batting average and a .367 on-base percentage.

The Infield and Designated Hitter

Catcher – Buster Posey. The only active player to make the team, Gerald (aka Buster) "pocket full of" Posey already has more hits than any other catcher with a flora name. His [1,005] hits and counting, [116] (soon to be more) home runs and [.307] lifetime batting average make him a welcome addition.

First Base – Mike Ivie. With a floral designation of ivy, you would expect this evergreen-climbing, woody plant to have played his career for the Cubs. However, Mike played for the

Padres and Giants, finishing his career with a respectable 724 hits, .269 batting average and .324 on-base percentage.

Second Base – Jody Reed. I took a tall slender-leaved plant at second base in the namesake Jody Reed. Reed gets plucked over Jake Flowers. Reed finished his career with 1231 hits, a respectable .270 batting average and an on base percentage of .349.

Shortstop – Donie Bush. Donie played from 1908 to1923 for the Washington Senators and Detroit Tigers and, simply put, was the best bush ever to play in the Big Leagues. He amassed 1,804 hits, with a .250 batting average and .356 on-base percentage. The inclusion of Sid Fernandez (as a fern) on the pitching staff eliminated shortstop Tony Fernandez from consideration.

Third Base – Pete Rose. Luckily for this Flora Team, the all-time hits leader played so many positions. During his career, Rose played all three outfield positions, second base, third base and first base and made the National League All-Star Team at all of these positions except center field. With 4,256 career hits, a .303 batting average and a .375 on-base percentage, Rose is a worthy member of this team and arguably its best position player.

DH – Graig Nettles. A nettle is not only a prickly or stinging plant but also, in this case, a Gold Glove third baseman that spent some time as a DH and was known to sting an opposing pitcher or two. Nettles finished his career with 2,225 hits, 390 home runs, 1,314 RBIs and a .248 batting average.

Bonus Selection – The Manager

Manager – Cum Posey. I've repeated a name here (no offense, Buster), but for good reason. This Hall of Famer got the nod as manager. From his Hall of Fame biography:

"First as a player and then later as manager and team owner, Cumberland Cum Posey was for 35 years the driving force behind the Homestead Grays, one of the most successful teams in Negro League history. His business acumen and organizational skills made the Grays a perennial powerhouse and money-making machine. He also had a keen eye for picking and developing talent, with more than 10 Negro League Hall of Famers playing for Posey's Homestead squad. During his tenure at the helm, Homestead split its home games between Pittsburgh and Washington, D.C., regularly drawing 25,000 to 30,000 fans to contests at Forbes Field and Griffith Stadium. Posey's team won eight of nine Negro National League pennants from 1937 to 1945, including three world titles."

Chapter Eight
The All-Time Body Part Team

Overview

For a player to be considered for this team, either the spelling of his first or last name must contain a human body part (sorry, anyone named Gil) and be its own syllable or the pronunciation of the player's name must match that of a human body part. For example, Ed Armbrister contains the body part "arm" as its own syllable, while John Hart's surname is pronounced like the body part "heart."

A name like Earl, while containing the body part "ear" in its spelling, is excluded because "ear" is not its own syllable in the name. Similarly, the name Morgan includes "organ" but is not considered for the team. However, a name like Early is eligible, since some pronounce it "Ear-Lee" instead of "Ur-Lee."

Slang terms for body parts (most notably, the defining part of the male anatomy and the rear extremity) are not considered for this team. The latter restriction rules out, for instance, Bud Heine, Josh Booty and Paul Assenmacher. However, words such as "bottom," to which Webster's dictionary assigns a body part definition (here, buttocks) can be considered (you're welcome, Jim Bottomley).

With players with first names like Armando, I could not resist allowing the use of first names for this team.

Fun Facts
- At least 48 unique human body parts are represented in Major League history by over 300 players in total.

- Body parts represented in the Hall of Fame include the palm (Jim Palmer), fingers (Rollie Fingers), heart (Gaby Hartnett) and bottom/buttocks (Jim Bottomley).
- The heart is the most common body part, with at least 68 players, thus proving that to make it in the Major Leagues you gotta have heart. The next most common body parts are the chest (thanks to the name Chester) and arm, with at least 25 references each.
- Rollie Fingers accounts for the only finger, and he is in the Hall of Fame.
- There is only one bottom (Jim Bottomley), a couple of butts (Ed Butka and Bill Butland), four Colons (Cris, Christian, Bartolo and Roman) and one anus, which admittedly may be a stretch of the team's eligibility guidelines (Bill Annis).
- Jake Eisenhart has the distinction of representing two body parts – eyes and heart – as does Rube Ehrhardt (Ear and Heart).

Thought Process on Team Selection

This was one of the toughest teams to assemble, as the pool of players is fairly limited when trying not to repeat a body part. While the initial list was slightly over 300 players, only five body parts accounted for half of those players. The initial list included the following players/body parts:

Body Part Player	Position	Years Active	Body Part
Bill Annis	CF	1884-1884	Anus
Armando Almanza	P	1999-2005	Arm
Tony Armas	P	1999-2008	Arm
Tony Armas	CF	1976-1989	Arm
Marcos Armas	1B	1993-1993	Arm
Ed Armbrister	LF	1973-1977	Arm

Body Part Player	Position	Years Active	Body Part
Orville Armbrust	P	1934-1934	Arm
Charlie Armbruster	C	1905-1907	Arm
Harry Armbruster	CF	1906-1906	Arm
Howard Armstrong	P	1911-1911	Arm
Jack Armstrong	P	1988-1994	Arm
Mike Armstrong	P	1980-1987	Arm
George Armstrong	C	1946-1946	Arm
Robert Armstrong	CF	1871-1871	Arm
Shawn Armstrong	P	2015-2015	Arm
Armando Benitez	P	1994-2008	Arm
Armand Cardoni	P	1943-1945	Arm
Charlie DeArmond	3B	1903-1903	Arm
Armando Gabino	P	2009-2010	Arm
Armando Galarraga	P	2007-2012	Arm
Armando Marsans	CF	1911-1918	Arm
Armando Reynoso	P	1991-2002	Arm
Armando Rios	RF	1998-2003	Arm
Armando Roche	P	1945-1945	Arm
Armando Romero	C	1997-2003	Arm
Armstrong Smith	OF	1912-1912	Arm
Rick Auerbach	SS	1971-1981	Back
Brandon Backe	P	2002-2009	Back
Les Backman	P	1909-1910	Back
Wally Backman	2B	1980-1993	Back
Dave Bakenhaster	P	1964-1964	Back
Jersey Bakley	P	1883-1891	Back
Paul Bako	C	1998-2009	Back
Frank Berkelbach	LF	1884-1884	Back
Bill Burbach	P	1969-1971	Back
Nick Koback	C	1953-1955	Back

Body Part Player	Position	Years Active	Body Part
Scottie Slayback	2B	1926-1926	Back
Bill Slayback	P	1972-1974	Back
Tuck Stainback	OF	1934-1946	Back
Bill Swarback	P	1887-1887	Back
Red Tramback	OF	1940-1940	Back
Rafael Belliard	SS	1982-1998	Belly
Ronnie Belliard	2B	1998-2010	Belly
Jimmy Bloodworth	2B	1937-1951	Blood
Chief Youngblood	P	1922-1922	Blood
Joel Youngblood	RF	1976-1989	Blood
George Bone	SS	1901-1901	Bone
Ricky Bones	P	1991-2001	Bone
Julio Bonetti	P	1937-1940	Bone
Hank Boney	P	1927-1927	Bone
Luther Bonin	RF	1913-1914	Bone
Jay Pettibone	P	1983-1983	Bone
Dave Brain	3B	1901-1908	Brain
Asa Brainard	P	1871-1874	Brain
Fred Brainard	1B	1914-1916	Brain
Scott Brow	P	1993-1998	Brow
Jim Bottomley	1B	1922-1937	Buttocks
Ed Butka	1B	1943-1944	Buttocks
Bill Butland	P	1940-1947	Buttocks
Tom Metcalf	P	1963-1963	Calf
Travis Metcalf	3B	2007-2008	Calf
Alfred Metcalfe	3B	1875-1875	Calf
Mike Metcalfe	LF	1998-2000	Calf
Harry Cheek	C	1910-1910	Cheek
Chet Boak	2B	1960-1961	Chest
Chick Brandom	P	1908-1915	Chest
Chester Carmichael	P	1909-1909	Chest

Body Part Player	Position	Years Active	Body Part
Chester Chadbourne	CF	1906-1918	Chest
Chester Clemens	LF	1939-1944	Chest
Chester Covington	P	1944-1944	Chest
Chester Crist	C	1906-1906	Chest
Chester Emerson	RF	1911-1912	Chest
Chester Falk	P	1925-1927	Chest
Chester Hajduk	PH	1941-1941	Chest
Chester Hoff	P	1911-1915	Chest
Chester Johnson	P	1946-1946	Chest
Chester Kehn	P	1942-1942	Chest
Chester Laabs	LF	1937-1947	Chest
Chester Lemon	CF	1975-1990	Chest
Chester Morgan	CF	1935-1938	Chest
Chester Nichols	P	1926-1932	Chest
Chester Nichols	P	1951-1964	Chest
Chester Nourse	P	1909-1909	Chest
Chester Poindexter	P	1936-1939	Chest
Chester Ross	P	1924-1926	Chest
Chester Ross	LF	1939-1944	Chest
Chester Spencer	OF	1906-1906	Chest
Chester Stephenson	P	1971-1978	Chest
Chester Thomas	C	1912-1921	Chest
ChesterTorkelson	P	1917-1917	Chest
Chin-Feng Chen	LF	2002-2005	Chin
Mike Milchin	P	1996-1996	Chin
Chien-Ming Wang	P	2005-2013	Chin
Bartolo Colon	P	1997-2015	Colon
Christian Colon	2B	2014-2015	Colon
Cris Colon	SS	1992-1992	Colon
Roman Colon	P	2004-2012	Colon
Arnold Earley	P	1960-1967	Ear

Body Part Player	Position	Years Active	Body Part
Tom Earley	P	1938-1945	Ear
Bill Earley	P	1986-1986	Ear
Jake Early	C	1939-1949	Ear
Eddie Eayrs	LF	1913-1921	Ear
Rube Ehrhardt	P	1924-1929	Ear
Dave Eiland	P	1988-2000	Eye
Dave Eilers	P	1964-1967	Eye
Jim Eisenreich	RF	1982-1998	Eye
Harry Eisenstat	P	1935-1942	Eye
Scott Eyre	P	1997-2009	Eye
Willie Eyre	P	2006-2011	Eye
George Eyrich	P	1943-1943	Eye
Jake Eisenhart	P	1944-1944	Eyes and Heart
Roy Face	P	1953-1969	Face
Rollie Fingers	RP	1968-1985	Finger
Doug Fister	P	2009-2015	Fist
Dan Pfister	P	1961-1964	Fist
George Pfister	C	1941-1941	Fist
Clyde Barfoot	P	1922-1926	Foot
Barry Foote	C	1973-1982	Foot
Don Gullett	P	1970-1978	Gullet
Jerry Hairston	LF	1973-1989	Hair
Jerry Hairston	2B	1998-2013	Hair
John Hairston	C	1969-1969	Hair
Sam Hairston	C	1951-1951	Hair
Scott Hairston	LF	2004-2014	Hair
Shawn Hare	LF	1991-1995	Hair
Bryan LaHair	1B	2008-2012	Hair
Brad Hand	P	2011-2015	Hand
Donovan Hand	P	2013-2015	Hand

Body Part Player	Position	Years Active	Body Part
Rich Hand	P	1970-1973	Hand
Mike Handiboe	OF	1911-1911	Hand
Jim Handiboe	P	1886-1886	Hand
Gene Handley	2B	1946-1947	Hand
Lee Handley	3B	1936-1947	Hand
Vern Handrahan	P	1964-1966	Hand
Bill Hands	P	1965-1975	Hand
Dan Bankhead	P	1947-1951	Head
Scott Bankhead	P	1986-1995	Head
Howard Craghead	P	1931-1933	Head
Ed Head	P	1940-1946	Head
Jerad Head	LF	2011-2011	Head
Ralph Head	P	1923-1923	Head
Chase Headley	3B	2007-2015	Head
Mike Hedlund	P	1965-1972	Head
Holly Hollingshead	CF	1872-1875	Head
Harry Lochhead	SS	1899-1901	Head
Bob Moorhead	P	1962-1965	Head
Dave Morehead	P	1963-1970	Head
Seth Morehead	P	1957-1961	Head
Burgess Whitehead	2B	1933-1946	Head
John Whitehead	P	1935-1942	Head
Milt Whitehead	SS	1884-1884	Head
Red Woodhead	3B	1873-1879	Head
Nick Adenhart	P	2008-2009	Heart
Clyde Barnhart	LF	1920-1928	Heart
Edgar Barnhart	P	1924-1924	Heart
Les Barnhart	P	1928-1930	Heart
Tucker Barnhart	C	2014-2015	Heart
Vic Barnhart	SS	1944-1946	Heart
Juan Bernhardt	DH	1976-1979	Heart

Body Part Player	Position	Years Active	Body Part
Walter Bernhardt	P	1918-1918	Heart
Jim Brillheart	P	1922-1931	Heart
Ken Burkhart	P	1945-1949	Heart
Morgan Burkhart	1B	2000-2003	Heart
John Buzhardt	P	1958-1968	Heart
Rick DeHart	P	1997-2003	Heart
Gary Gearhart	CF	1947-1947	Heart
Rusty Gerhardt	P	1974-1974	Heart
Joe Gerhardt	2B	1873-1891	Heart
Ken Gerhart	CF	1986-1988	Heart
Bo Hart	2B	2003-2004	Heart
Hub Hart	C	1905-1907	Heart
Jimmy Hart	1B	1901-1901	Heart
Mike Hart	CF	1980-1980	Heart
Jim Ray Hart	3B	1963-1974	Heart
Jason Hart	1B	2002-2002	Heart
Corey Hart	1B	2004-2015	Heart
Kevin Hart	P	2007-2009	Heart
Mike Hart	CF	1984-1987	Heart
Billy Hart	P	1890-1890	Heart
Tom Hart	C	1891-1891	Heart
Bill Hart	P	1886-1901	Heart
Bill Hart	3B	1943-1945	Heart
Chuck Hartenstein	P	1965-1977	Heart
Frank Harter	P	1912-1914	Heart
Bruce Hartford	SS	1914-1914	Heart
Dean Hartgraves	P	1995-1998	Heart
Jumbo Harting	C	1886-1886	Heart
Chris Hartje	C	1939-1939	Heart
Grover Hartley	C	1911-1934	Heart
Mike Hartley	P	1989-1995	Heart

Body Part Player	Position	Years Active	Body Part
Chick Hartley	LF	1902-1902	Heart
Charlie Hartman	P	1908-1908	Heart
Fred Hartman	3B	1894-1902	Heart
J C Hartman	SS	1962-1963	Heart
Bob Hartman	P	1959-1962	Heart
Gabby Hartnett	C	1922-1941	Heart
Pat Hartnett	1B	1890-1890	Heart
Ray Hartranft	P	1913-1913	Heart
Greg Harts	PH	1973-1973	Heart
Topsy Hartsel	LF	1898-1911	Heart
Roy Hartsfield	2B	1950-1952	Heart
Jeff Hartsock	P	1992-1992	Heart
Clint Hartung	P	1947-1952	Heart
Paul Hartzell	P	1976-1984	Heart
Roy Hartzell	3B	1906-1916	Heart
Don Lenhardt	LF	1950-1954	Heart
Glenn Liebhardt	P	1930-1938	Heart
Glenn Liebhardt	P	1906-1909	Heart
Carl Linhart	PH	1952-1952	Heart
Keith Lockhart	2B	1994-2003	Heart
Paul Menhart	P	1995-1997	Heart
John Mohardt	OF	1922-1922	Heart
George Mohart	P	1920-1921	Heart
Ray Morehart	2B	1924-1927	Heart
Moe Morhardt	1B	1961-1962	Heart
Rick Reichardt	LF	1964-1974	Heart
Art Reinhart	P	1919-1928	Heart
Mike Richardt	2B	1980-1984	Heart
Blake Swihart	LF	2015-2015	Heart
Robbie Weinhardt	P	2010-2011	Heart
Fran Healy	C	1969-1978	Heel

Body Part Player	Position	Years Active	Body Part
Francis Healy	C	1930-1934	Heel
Egyptian Healy	P	1885-1892	Heel
Thomas Healy	3B	1915-1916	Heel
Hipolito Pena	P	1986-1988	Hip
Hipolito Pichardo	P	1992-2002	Hip
Herb Hippauf	P	1966-1966	Hip
Adrian Nieto	C	2014-2014	Knee
Tom Nieto	C	1984-1990	Knee
Fernando Nieve	P	2006-2010	Knee
Jose Nieves	SS	1998-2002	Knee
Juan Nieves	P	1986-1988	Knee
Melvin Nieves	RF	1992-1998	Knee
Wil Nieves	C	2002-2015	Knee
George Pinkney	3B	1884-1893	Knee
Johnny Podgajny	P	1940-1946	Knee
Jack Lapp	C	1908-1916	Lap
Lou Legett	C	1929-1935	Leg
Greg Legg	2B	1986-1987	Leg
Jim Haislip	P	1913-1913	Lip
Johnny Lipon	SS	1942-1954	Lip
Tom Lipp	P	1897-1897	Lip
Nig Lipscomb	2B	1937-1937	Lip
Bob Lipski	C	1963-1963	Lip
Lip Pike	CF	1871-1887	Lip
Ed Amelung	RF	1984-1986	Lung
Buck Marrow	P	1932-1938	Marrow
Jeff Musselman	P	1986-1990	Muscle
Ron Musselman	P	1982-1985	Muscle
Jackie Collum	P	1951-1962	Neck
Randy Nosek	P	1989-1990	Nose
Joe Nossek	CF	1964-1970	Nose

Body Part Player	Position	Years Active	Body Part
Mike Overy	P	1976-1976	Ovary
Paul LaPalme	P	1951-1957	Palm
Mike Palm	P	1948-1948	Palm
Orlando Palmeiro	LF	1995-2007	Palm
Rafael Palmeiro	1B	1986-2005	Palm
Billy Palmer	P	1885-1885	Palm
David Palmer	P	1978-1989	Palm
Dean Palmer	3B	1989-2003	Palm
Eddie Palmer	3B	1917-1917	Palm
Jim Palmer	P	1965-1984	Palm
Matt Palmer	P	2008-2012	Palm
Lowell Palmer	P	1969-1974	Palm
Emilio Palmero	P	1915-1928	Palm
Joe Palmisano	C	1931-1931	Palm
Ed Palmquist	P	1960-1961	Palm
Palmer Hildebrand	C	1913-1913	Palm
Luke Prokopec	P	2000-2002	Pec
Skip Pitlock	P	1970-1975	Pit
Chris Pittaro	3B	1985-1987	Pit
Pinky Pittenger	SS	1921-1929	Pit
Togie Pittinger	P	1900-1907	Pit
Joe Pittman	2B	1981-1984	Pit
Gaylen Pitts	3B	1974-1975	Pit
Jim Pittsley	P	1995-1999	Pit
Stan Pitula	P	1957-1957	Pit
Herman Pitz	C	1890-1890	Pit
Jeff Reardon	P	1979-1994	Rear
Jeremiah Reardon	P	1886-1886	Rear
Phil Reardon	RF	1906-1906	Rear
Chris Rearick	P	2015-2015	Rear
Dennis Ribant	P	1964-1969	Rib

Body Part Player	Position	Years Active	Body Part
Harvey Shank	P	1970-1970	Shank
Howie Shanks	OF	1912-1925	Shank
Shin-Soo Choo	RF	2005-2015	Shin
Ralph Shinners	OF	1922-1925	Shin
Tim Shinnick	2B	1890-1891	Shin
Zak Shinall	P	1993-1993	Shin
Ginger Shinault	C	1921-1922	Shin
Billy Shindle	3B	1886-1898	Shin
Tsuyoshi Shinjo	CF	2001-2003	Shin
Shingo Takatsu	P	2004-2005	Shin
Al Skinner	OF	1884-1884	Skin
Camp Skinner	OF	1922-1923	Skin
Joel Skinner	C	1983-1991	Skin
Bob Skinner	LF	1954-1966	Skin
Dave Thies	P	1963-1963	Thighs
Jake Thies	P	1954-1955	Thighs
Hal Toenes	P	1947-1947	Toe
Bobby Tolan	OF	1965-1979	Toe

The best players tended to share the same body part. For example, Jim Palmer and Rafael Palmeiro share the palm.

The use of body parts represented in the Hall of Fame eliminates further use of Bottom, Heart, Palm and Fingers – and thus removes approximately 50 players from the remaining pool.

Figuring Gaby Hartnett a lock for catcher, I then removed all 14 other catchers from my list of available players.

With a remaining pool of around 105 players to select four starting pitchers and all position players except catcher, I began removing all players who played no more than a couple of years in the Majors, then started to make a short list by body part, which pared my list down to 28 players. Upon further inspection, I could see that I had no candidates for first base. When I looked at the body parts still represented on my list, I knew I would have to make a tough choice. My remaining pool of 28 players included five arms and one brain, so selecting a brain for first base eliminated just one from my pool, versus eliminating four from the pool by selecting an arm. I would have to evaluate whether an arm player could fill another position before making my final decision.

I then lined up all of my 13 available pitchers. One of them, Armando Benitez, was used exclusively as a closer. While he was a good one (Mets fans may disagree), he was no Rollie Fingers, so I felt safe eliminating Benitez from my list. That left me with the following 12 pitchers: Tony Arm(as), Arm(ando) Reynoso, Brandon Back(e), Ricky Bones, Chest(er) Nichols, Chien (Chin)-Ming Wang, Roy Face, Don Gullett, Bill Hands, Ed Head, Hip(olito) Pichardo and Jeff Mussel(muscle)man.

I also lined up my remaining position players: Tony Arm(as), Arm(ando) Rios, Wally Back(man), Ronnie Belliard (Belly), Jimmy Bloodworth, Joel Youngblood, Dave Brain, Chest(er) Lemon, Jerry Hair(ston), Lee Hand(ley), Chase Head(ley), Johnny Lip(on), Billy Shin(dle), Shin-(Soo) Choo, Bob Skin(ner).

With the above lists in hand, my final approach was to compare statistics and identify the best four remaining pitchers and the best position players – and see if any of the top position players could qualify for first base, amid so few candidates.

The Final Team

The Pitching Staff

Starting Pitcher 1 – Jim Palmer. Jim's 268 career wins (against 152 losses), 2.86 ERA and 1.18 WHIP explain why he is in the Hall of Fame.

Starting Pitcher 2 – Bartolo Colon. While not the most flattering part of the body, it is still nonetheless an important one. Colon is an active body part pitcher, whose [233] career wins (and counting) rank him behind only Jim Palmer on the body part list. His 3.93 ERA and 1.33 WHIP make Colon a great number two starter for this team.

Starting Pitcher 3 – Don Gullett. Don "the esophagus/gullet" Gullett was an easy choice as my third starter, as his career .685 winning percentage (109 – 50) was better than all of the other candidates. His career 3.11 ERA was also easy to swallow.

Starting Pitcher 4 – Bill Hands. This team is certainly in good Hands with Bill. Bill's 111 career wins leads all body part pitchers not named Jim Palmer or Bartolo Colon. While his 110 career losses also lead all body part pitchers not named Jim Palmer and Bartolo Colon, his career 3.35 ERA is what makes him an integral part of the All-Time Body Part Team.

Starting Pitcher 5 – Chien-Ming Wang. Moving from the Hands to part of the face, Chien (Chin) makes the team as a current Major League player. While arm injuries have negatively impacted his career, I could not pass up his career

.667 winning percentage (68-34). He got the nod over Roy Face, who was primarily a reliever.

Closer – Rollie Fingers. I hate to give my readers the finger, but in this case I had no choice but to add Hall of Fame relief pitcher Rollie Fingers to this team. Fingers ranks 11th all-time with 341 saves, to go along with 114 career wins and a 2.90 ERA. Of those 10 relief pitchers with more saves than Fingers, only Dennis Eckersley has more wins.

The Outfield
Center Field – Chester (aka "Chet") Lemon. Let's all pound our chests for Chest(er) Lemon. Although nicknamed "the Jet," Lemon finished his career with only 58 stolen bases. He did, however, have 1,875 hits, 215 home runs, a .273 batting average and a .355 on-base percentage.

Right Field – Shin-Soo Choo. Current Big Leaguer Shin-Soo Choo got a leg up on his closest competition for this spot, Jim Eisenreich. Through the first [1,173] games of his career, Choo has amassed [1,206] hits and [146] home runs, hitting .280 with a .381 on-base percentage.

Left Field – Bob Skinner. The skin is the largest organ in the human body, and Bob Skinner fits right in on the All-Time Body Part Team. Bob collected 1,198 career hits, with 103 home runs, a .277 batting average and a .351 on-base percentage.

The Infield and Designated Hitter

Catcher – Gaby Hartnett. This hearty Hall of Famer showed a lot of heart during his career, so he makes this team. He also totaled 1,912 hits, 236 home runs, a .297 batting average and a .370 on-base percentage.

First Base – Jim Bottomley. Bringing up the rear is our third Hall of Famer to make the team. Bottomley totaled 2,313 hits, 219 home runs, a .310 batting average and a .369 on-base percentage. In 1,991 career games, mostly with the St. Louis Browns, Bottomley amassed more walks (664) than strikeouts (591).

Second Base – Wally Backman. The back is an important part of the body for a hitter, so it is only fitting to ensure its representation on the All-Time Body Part Team. Backman got the nod over Ronnie Belliard (representing the belly, of course) even though Belliard led Backman in many offensive categories. That said, Backman led Belliard in stolen bases (117 vs. 43), batting average (.275 vs. .273) and on-base percentage (.349 vs. .338). As such, I decided to take Backman but certainly could have gone either way – and James Bloodworth and Burgess Whitehead also merited consideration.

Shortstop – Johnny Lipon. This lip beats out another belly (Rafael Belliard) as the starting shortstop. Lipon amassed 690 career hits, with a .259 batting average and .346 on-base percentage.

Third Base – Chase Headley. A body and a team both need a head, so I picked current player Chase Headley as this team's third baseman. The selection of Shin-Soo Choo eliminated Billy Shindle from the team. In his first [1,262] games, Headley has [1,191] hits, [118] home runs, [84] stolen bases, a [.263] batting average and a [.343] on-base percentage.

DH – Tony Armas. I opted to add some power with the final spot on the team. Not to be confused with his son the pitcher (who took his "arm" name more literally, I guess), this Armas played primarily as an outfielder for the A's, Red Sox and Angels (although his career began with a brief stint with the Pirates). In 1,432 career games, the senior Armas hit 251 home runs while batting .252. His career .287 on-base percentage does not earn him fans among moneyball proponents, but he's armed and ready for this team.

Chapter Nine
The All-Time Financial Team

Overview

When investing your (Don) Money in a (Milt) Stock, wait for the (Buddy) Bell of the exchange to sound, then buy (Derek) Lowe and sell (Andy) High. Make sure you get your (Barry) Bonds at the right (Dave) Price or invest in a mutual (Lee) Pfund. Don't execute a (Bill) Short (Chris) Sale, as it's better to go (Ryan) Long in your investments. When you make a (Brad) Penny, or even better a couple of (Kid) Nichols, you can save your hard-earned (Dave) Cash in the (Ernie) Bank(s) to earn a few extra (Curt) Schilling(s) and pay off your (Mike) Loan early.

To make this team, the player's surname needs to contain a clearly pronounced financial term. My apologies to the (Ernie) Wolf of Wall Street, as the eligible financial terms are limited to the following 80:

Asset	Dime	Gain	Offer	Sell
Bank	Dinero	Income	Option	Sellers
Bell	Dollar	Index	Pence	Shares
Bear	Earn	Keogh	Penny	Short
Bond	Earnings	Leap	Pension	Silver
Bull	Equity	Lend	Poor	Stock
Buy	Euro	Lien	Price	Swap
Buyers	Float	Lira	Profit	Trade
Call	Fund	Loan	Puts	Turnover
Capital	Future	Long	Quarter	Uptick
Cash	Gold	Low	Rally	Value

Coin	Goodwill	Margin	Rate	Warrant
Cost	Greenback	Market	Rich	Will
Credit	Handle	Merger	Risk	Worth
Currency	Hedge	Money	Sale	Wire
Debt	High	Nickel	Schilling	Yield

Fun Facts

- Only 39 of the 80 financial terms have been represented in professional baseball history.
- Kid Nichols (pronounced "nickels"), Ernie Banks and Dave Bancroft are the financially named Hall of Famers to have played in the Major Leagues. Negro League star James "Cool Papa" Bell is also a Hall of Famer with a financial-related surname.
- Barry Bonds is the all-time financial leader in hits (2,935), home runs (762) and walks (2,558).
- Tommy Bond leads all financial pitchers with a career 2.25 ERA. Kid Nichols is second with a 2.95 ERA.
- Financial hitters on the all-time top 500 list of career batting averages include Barry Bonds (.298), Billy Southworth (.297), Albert Belle (.295), Troy Tulowitzski [update before publishing?] and Milt Stock (.289), Andy High (.284), Dave Cash (.283) and Maury Wills (.281).
- Bell is the most popular financial name, with at least 27 players named Bell and one each named Belle and Bellhorn.
- Gold leads the Majors among precious metals, with at least 11 players to have Gold in their names (Golden, Goldman, Goldsberry, Goldsmith, Goldstein, Goldy, Goldschmidt). At least four variations of Silver have played in the Big Leagues (Silverio and Silvera).

- The Major Leagues have multiple bulls (Danny and Jose Tartabull) but only one bear (Doug Bair).

Thought Process on Team Selection

The main challenge in forming the All-Time Financial Team was filling the entire roster without repeating a term. My initial scan of players matching any of the 80 eligible financial terms yielded the following 280 players:

Last Name	First	Position	Years Active	Financial Term
Bancker	Studs	C	1875-1875	Bank
Banks	Ernie	SS	1953-1971	Bank
Bancroft	Dave	SS	1915-1930	Bank
Banks	Willie	P	1991-2002	Bank
Bankhead	Scott	P	1986-1995	Bank
Banks	Brian	LF	1996-2003	Bank
Banks	George	3B	1962-1966	Bank
Bankhead	Dan	P	1947-1951	Bank
Banks	Josh	P	2007-2010	Bank
Eubank	John	P	1905-1907	Bank
Fairbank	Jim	P	1903-1904	Bank
Bankston	Bill	OF	1915-1915	Bank
Eubanks	Uel	P	1922-1922	Bank
Bankston	Wes	1B	2008-2008	Bank
Bair	Doug	P	1976-1990	Bear
Bell	Charlie	P	1889-1891	Bell
Bell	Frank	C	1885-1885	Bell
Bell	Buddy	3B	1972-1989	Bell
Bell	Jay	SS	1986-2003	Bell

Last Name	First	Position	Years Active	Financial Term
Bell	Gus	CF	1950-1964	Bell
Bell	George	LF	1981-1993	Bell
Bell	David	3B	1995-2006	Bell
Bell	Gary	P	1958-1969	Bell
Belle	Albert	LF	1989-2000	Bell
Bell	Hi	P	1924-1934	Bell
Bellhorn	Mark	2B	1997-2007	Bell
Bell	Derek	RF	1991-2001	Bell
Bell	Heath	P	2004-2014	Bell
Bell	Les	3B	1923-1931	Bell
Bell	Eric	P	1985-1993	Bell
Bell	Rob	P	2000-2007	Bell
Bell	Beau	RF	1935-1941	Bell
Bell	Kevin	3B	1976-1982	Bell
Bell	Juan	2B	1989-1995	Bell
Bell	Trevor	P	2009-2014	Bell
Bell	George	P	1907-1911	Bell
Belloir	Rob	SS	1975-1978	Bell
Bell	Jerry	P	1971-1974	Bell
Bell	Bill	P	1952-1955	Bell
Bella	Zeke	RF	1957-1959	Bell
Bell	Josh	3B	2010-2012	Bell
Bellorin	Edwin	C	2007-2009	Bell
Bell	Mike	1B	1990-1991	Bell
Bell	Fern	CF	1939-1940	Bell
Bell	Terry	C	1986-1987	Bell
Bell	Mike	3B	2000-2000	Bell
Bell	Rudy	LF	1907-1907	Bell
Bell	Ralph	P	1912-1912	Bell
Bond	Tommy	P	1874-1884	Bond

Last Name	First	Position	Years Active	Financial Term
Bonds	Barry	LF	1986-2007	Bond
Bonds	Bobby	RF	1968-1981	Bond
Bonderman	Jeremy	P	2003-2013	Bond
Bond	Walt	1B	1960-1967	Bond
Trumbull	Ed	OF	1884-1884	Bull
Tartabull	Danny	OF	1984-1997	Bull
Tartabull	Jose	CF	1962-1970	Bull
Byers	Randy	OF	1987-1988	Buyer
Byers	Bill	C	1904-1904	Buyer
McCall	Windy	P	1948-1957	Call
McCall	Larry	P	1977-1979	Call
McCall	Brian	RF	1962-1963	Call
McCall	Dutch	P	1948-1948	Call
Cash	Norm	1B	1958-1974	Cash
Cash	Dave	2B	1969-1980	Cash
Cash	Kevin	C	2002-2010	Cash
Cash	Ron	1B	1973-1974	Cash
Kashiwada	Takashi	P	1997-1997	Cash
Aucoin	Derek	P	1996-1996	Coin
Coyne	Toots	3B	1914-1914	Coin
Coste	Chris	C	2006-2009	Cost
Costo	Tim	RF	1992-1993	Cost
Earnshaw	George	P	1928-1936	Earn
Pfund	Lee	P	1945-1945	Fund
Gainer	Del	1B	1909-1922	Gain
Gaines	Joe	RF	1960-1966	Gain
Gainey	Ty	CF	1985-1987	Gain
Gainer	Jay	1B	1993-1993	Gain
Gaines	Nemo	P	1921-1921	Gain
Golden	Mike	P	1875-1878	Gold

Last Name	First	Position	Years Active	Financial Term
Goldsby	Walt	OF	1884-1888	Gold
Goldsmith	Fred	P	1875-1884	Gold
Goldsmith	Wally	3B	1871-1875	Gold
Goldschmidt	Paul	1B	2011-2015	Gold
Goldsberry	Gordon	1B	1949-1952	Gold
Goldsmith	Hal	P	1926-1929	Gold
Goldstein	Lon	1B	1943-1946	Gold
Goldman	Jonah	SS	1928-1931	Gold
Golden	Jim	P	1960-1963	Gold
Goldy	Purnal	RF	1962-1963	Gold
Golden	Roy	P	1910-1911	Gold
Goldstein	Izzy	P	1932-1932	Gold
High	Andy	3B	1922-1934	High
High	Hugh	LF	1913-1918	High
High	Charlie	RF	1919-1920	High
High	Ed	P	1901-1901	High
Held	Woodie	SS	1954-1969	Hold
Barthold	John	P	1904-1904	Hold
Held	Mel	P	1956-1956	Hold
Keough	Marty	CF	1956-1966	Keough
Keough	Matt	P	1977-1986	Keough
Keough	Joe	RF	1968-1973	Keough
Lira	Felipe	P	1995-2001	Lira
Lown	Turk	P	1951-1962	Loan
Loney	James	1B	2006-2015	Loan
Meloan	Jon	P	2007-2009	Loan
Meloan	Paul	RF	1910-1911	Loan
Loane	Bob	CF	1939-1940	Loan
Loun	Don	P	1964-1964	Loan
Loan	Mike	C	1912-1912	Loan

Last Name	First	Position	Years Active	Financial Term
Long	Dan	CF	1890-1890	Long
Long	Herman	SS	1889-1904	Long
Long	Jim	OF	1891-1893	Long
Long	Thomas	RF	1888-1888	Long
Long	Dale	1B	1951-1963	Long
Long	Terrence	CF	1999-2006	Long
Long	Tom	RF	1911-1917	Long
Long	Bill	P	1985-1991	Long
Long	Bob	P	1981-1985	Long
Long	Jeoff	1B	1963-1964	Long
Long	Joey	P	1997-1997	Long
Long	Jimmie	C	1922-1922	Long
Long	Lep	P	1911-1911	Long
Long	Ryan	RF	1997-1997	Long
Long	Red	P	1902-1902	Long
Long	Tom	P	1924-1924	Long
Lowe	Bobby	2B	1890-1907	Low
Lowe	Charlie	2B	1872-1872	Low
Lowe	Dick	C	1884-1884	Low
Lowe	Derek	P	1997-2013	Low
Kretlow	Lou	P	1946-1956	Low
Lowe	Mark	P	2006-2015	Low
Tulowitzki	Troy	SS	2006-2015	Low
Luplow	Al	RF	1961-1967	Low
Lowe	Sean	P	1997-2003	Low
Marlowe	Dick	P	1951-1956	Low
Lo	Chia-Jen	P	2013-2013	Low
Low	Fletcher	3B	1915-1915	Low
Lowe	George	P	1920-1920	Low
Money	Don	3B	1968-1983	Money

Last Name	First	Position	Years Active	Financial Term
Nicholl	Sam	LF	1888-1890	Nickel
Nichols	Al	3B	1875-1877	Nickel
Nichols	Art	C	1898-1903	Nickel
Nichols	Kid	P	1890-1906	Nickel
Nichols	Tricky	P	1875-1882	Nickel
Nicholson	Parson	2B	1888-1895	Nickel
Nicol	George	RF	1890-1894	Nickel
Nicol	Hugh	RF	1881-1890	Nickel
Nicholson	Bill	RF	1936-1953	Nickel
Nichols	Chet	P	1951-1964	Nickel
Nicholson	Dave	LF	1960-1967	Nickel
Nichols	Rod	P	1988-1995	Nickel
Nichols	Reid	CF	1980-1987	Nickel
Nicholls	Simon	SS	1903-1910	Nickel
Nichols	Chet	P	1926-1932	Nickel
Nicholson	Fred	LF	1917-1922	Nickel
Nichols	Carl	C	1986-1991	Nickel
Nickle	Doug	P	2000-2002	Nickel
Nichols	Dolan	P	1958-1958	Nickel
Nichols	Roy	2B	1944-1944	Nickel
Nicolino	Justin	P	2015-2015	Nickel
McNichol	Ed	P	1904-1904	Nickel
Nicholson	Kevin	SS	2000-2000	Nickel
McNichol	Brian	P	1999-1999	Nickel
Nicholson	Ovid	LF	1912-1912	Nickel
Nicholson	Frank	P	1912-1912	Nickel
Pence	Hunter	RF	2007-2015	Pence
Pence	Rusty	P	1921-1921	Pence
Pence	Elmer	RF	1922-1922	Pence
Penny	Brad	P	2000-2014	Penny

Last Name	First	Position	Years Active	Financial Term
Pennyfeather	Will	CF	1992-1994	Penny
Poorman	Tom	RF	1880-1888	Poor
Price	Bill	P	1890-1890	Price
Price	Joe	P	1980-1990	Price
Price	David	P	2008-2015	Price
Price	Jim	C	1967-1971	Price
Price	Jackie	SS	1946-1946	Price
Price	Bryan	P	2014-2014	Price
Price	Joe	CF	1928-1928	Price
Putz	J. J.	P	2003-2014	Puts
Richmond	John	SS	1875-1885	Rich
Richmond	Lee	P	1879-1886	Rich
Ritchey	Claude	2B	1897-1909	Rich
Ulrich	George	OF	1892-1896	Rich
Richert	Pete	P	1962-1974	Rich
Richbourg	Lance	RF	1921-1932	Rich
Richmond	Don	3B	1941-1951	Rich
Ritchie	Todd	P	1997-2004	Rich
Richie	Lew	P	1906-1913	Rich
Rich	Woody	P	1939-1944	Rich
Ritchie	Wally	P	1987-1992	Rich
Fidrych	Mark	P	1976-1980	Rich
Burich	Bill	SS	1942-1946	Rich
Ritchie	Jay	P	1964-1968	Rich
Richardt	Mike	2B	1980-1984	Rich
Richmond	Scott	P	2008-2012	Rich
Aldrich	Jay	P	1987-1990	Rich
Barberich	Frank	P	1907-1910	Rich
Ulrich	Dutch	P	1925-1927	Rich
Richar	Danny	2B	2007-2009	Rich

Last Name	First	Position	Years Active	Financial Term
Gertenrich	Lou	OF	1901-1903	Rich
Richmond	Beryl	P	1933-1934	Rich
Ullrich	Sandy	P	1944-1945	Rich
Emmerich	Slim	P	1945-1946	Rich
Richmond	Ray	P	1920-1921	Rich
Lovrich	Pete	P	1963-1963	Rich
Helfrich	Ty	2B	1915-1915	Rich
Richie	Rob	LF	1989-1989	Rich
Emmerich	Bob	CF	1923-1923	Rich
Riske	David	P	1999-2010	Risk
Sales	Ed	SS	1890-1890	Sale
Sale	Chris	P	2010-2015	Sale
Sale	Freddy	P	1924-1924	Sale
Schilling	Curt	P	1988-2007	Schilling
Schilling	Chuck	2B	1961-1965	Schilling
Shilling	Jim	2B	1939-1939	Schilling
Schillings	Red	P	1922-1922	Schilling
Sellman	Frank	C	1871-1875	Sell
Selkirk	George	OF	1934-1942	Sell
Sells	Dave	P	1972-1975	Sell
Whitesell	Josh	1B	2008-2009	Sell
Sell	Epp	P	1922-1923	Sell
Selbach	Kip	OF	1894-1906	Sell
Sellers	Justin	SS	2011-2014	Sellers
Sellers	Jeff	P	1985-1988	Sellers
Sellers	Rube	OF	1910-1910	Sellers
Short	Chris	P	1959-1973	Short
Short	Bill	P	1960-1969	Short
Shorten	Chick	OF	1915-1924	Short
Short	Dave	OF	1940-1941	Short

Last Name	First	Position	Years Active	Financial Term
Short	Rick	3B	2005-2005	Short
Silvera	Charlie	C	1948-1957	Silver
Silverio	Tom	CF	1970-1972	Silver
Silvera	Al	LF	1955-1956	Silver
Silverio	Luis	LF	1978-1978	Silver
Berkenstock	Nate	RF	1871-1871	Stock
Stocksdale	Otis	P	1893-1896	Stock
Stockwell	Len	C	1879-1890	Stock
Stock	Milt	3B	1913-1926	Stock
Stock	Wes	P	1959-1967	Stock
Comstock	Keith	P	1984-1991	Stock
Stocker	Kevin	SS	1993-2000	Stock
Comstock	Ralph	P	1913-1918	Stock
Bostock	Lyman	CF	1975-1978	Stock
Stockman	Phil	P	2006-2008	Stock
Estock	George	P	1951-1951	Stock
Stocker	Mel	LF	2007-2007	Stock
Wills	Dave	1B	1899-1899	Will
Wills	Maury	SS	1959-1972	Will
Wills	Frank	P	1983-1991	Will
Wills	Ted	P	1959-1965	Will
Wills	Bump	2B	1977-1982	Will
Cudworth	Jim		1884-1884	Worth
Holdsworth	Jim		1872-1884	Worth
Wadsworth	Jack		1890-1895	Worth
Wordsworth	Favel		1873-1873	Worth
Worth	Herb		1872-1872	Worth
Hayworth	Ray	C	1926-1945	Worth
Southworth	Billy	RF	1913-1929	Worth
Farnsworth	Kyle	P	1999-2014	Worth

Last Name	First	Position	Years Active	Financial Term
Werth	Jayson	LF	2002-2015	Worth
Ellsworth	Dick	P	1958-1971	Worth
Hollingsworth	Al	P	1935-1946	Worth
Hollandsworth	Todd	LF	1995-2006	Worth
Frohwirth	Todd	P	1987-1996	Worth
Holdsworth	Fred	P	1972-1980	Worth
Duckworth	Brandon	P	2001-2008	Worth
Hollingsworth	Bonnie	P	1922-1928	Worth
Wortham	Rich	P	1978-1983	Worth
Worth	Danny	2B	2010-2014	Worth
Duckworth	Jim	P	1963-1966	Worth
Werth	Dennis	1B	1979-1982	Worth
Allensworth	Jermaine	CF	1996-1999	Worth
Ainsworth	Kurt	P	2001-2004	Worth
Hawksworth	Blake	P	2009-2011	Worth
Hayworth	Red	C	1944-1945	Worth
Farnsworth	Jeff	P	2002-2002	Worth
Ellsworth	Steve	P	1988-1988	Worth
Skipworth	Kyle	C	2013-2013	Worth
Haworth	Howie	C	1915-1915	Worth
Southworth	Bill	3B	1964-1964	Worth

The above list includes 33 Bells, 29 Worths, 29 Riches, 26 Nickels, 16 Lows, 14 Banks and 13 Golds (or their respective variants). Taken together, these terms comprise more than half of the list of 280 available players. Selecting a bank and nickel from the Hall of Fame (Ernie Banks and Kid Nichols) immediately further reduced the available player pool. Removing all players with little to no experience and selecting all-time home run leader Barry Bonds also significantly shrank the available player universe. Limiting the list by position and selecting top players by term also dramatically filtered down the list.

When all of this was done, the original list of 280 became a more manageable list of 67.

The infield seemed to enjoy a lot of options, especially with players like Milt Stock, Don Money, Andy High and Ernie Banks having played multiple infield positions.

I also was encouraged by a reasonable-looking short list of pitchers. Potential starters beyond Kid Nichols were retired players Curt Schilling, Brad Penny, Derek Lowe and Chris Short, as well as current players such as David Price and Chris Sale. Relief pitchers included Doug Bair, Kyle Farnsworth and JJ Putz.

Filling out the outfield and finding a catcher required more diligence. The short list of catchers included Ray Hayworth, Charlie Silvera and Mike Loan.

The Final Team

The Pitching Staff

Starting Pitcher 1 – Kid Nichols. This Hall of Famer was worth more than nickels; in fact, he was the obvious choice as the Financial Team's top starter. Nichols finished his career with a record of 361 – 208 and a 2.95 ERA. He also saved 17 games, for good measure.

Starting Pitcher 2 – Curt Schilling. Schilling (or "shilling," in strictly financial terms) was certainly a money pitcher. In his career, he compiled 216 wins against 146 losses, along with a 3.46 ERA. His 3,116 strikeouts put him in the top 20 all-time.

Starting Pitcher 3 –David Price. There is nothing cheap about our Price, a currently active player with [121] wins against only [65] losses and a [3.21] ERA.

Starting Pitcher 4 – Chris Short. When you short a stock, you hope its price drops. However, no need to be down on Short, whose career mark of 135-132 and a 3.42 ERA qualified him for the Financial Team.

Starting Pitcher 5 – Brad Penny. I took Penny over Chris Sale based simply on longevity. I have no doubt Sale will make the team in the future but for now, Penny's 121-101 record and 4.29 ERA and cool monetary name make him a fit for this current incarnation of the All-Financial Team.

Honorable Mention: Chris Sale – Sale is sure to be an addition in the future if he continues his current pace. As of the end of the 2015 season, Sale had 74 wins against 50 loses and an ERA under 3.

Closer – JJ Putz (pronounced "Puts"). Thanks to the existence of a financial instrument called a "put" (which is an option to sell a stock at a specified price for a specified period), I was able to name Putz as this team's closer. In baseball terms, I granted him the spot based on his 189 career saves and more than a strikeout per inning.

The Outfield

Center Field – Kip Selbach ("sell back"). No need to sell back anything on this old-time player whose career spanned the years 1894 to 1906. Selbach finished with 1,803 hits, 334 stolen bases, a .293 batting average and a .376 on-base percentage.

Right Field – Hunter Pence. Pence, the English Penny, was another active player deserving a spot on this team. Pence currently sports a [.284] career batting average and a [.339] on-base percentage, with [207] home runs and [107] stolen bases.

Left Field – Barry Bonds. A bond is a financial instrument of indebtedness, and we baseball fans are all indebted to this particular Bond. Barry amassed 2,935 hits, 762 home runs, 514 stolen bases, a .298 career batting average and a .444 on-base percentage. Steroids or not, he is on this team.

The Infield and Designated Hitter

Catcher – Mike Loan. No need to pay anyone back, Mike. I selected Mike Loan over Ray Hayworth simply on the basis of who had the better name. Hayworth sounded too much like a movie starlet, so I opted for Loan's career .500 batting average and .500 on-base percentage. Of course, these statistics resulted from only two career at-bats (one of them a hit). Still, that name is one of the ultimate financial terms, no?

First Base – Norm Cash. In business, it is said that "cash is king." Therefore, I felt compelled to take this Cash. A career of 1,820 hits, 377 home runs, a .271 batting average and a .374 on-base percentage didn't hurt, either.

Second Base – Milt Stock. I took stock of Milt and decided to put him on this team somewhat out of position. While primarily a third baseman, Stock played both second base and shortstop as well, so I plugged him in at second. In his career, he had 1,806 hits, a .289 batting average (ranking him in the top 500) and a .339 on-base percentage.

Shortstop – Ernie Banks. Presented with an easy Hall of Famer pick for this team, I certainly felt safe with this Banks. While Ernie played a considerable portion of his career at first base, he also was the original power-hitting shortstop. In his career, he accumulated 512 home runs, 2,583 hits, a .274 batting average and a .330 on-base percentage.

Third Base – Don Money. You simply cannot have a financial team without Money. Don's 1,623 career hits, 176 home runs, .261 batting average and .328 on-base percentage made him a worthy financial addition.

DH – Buddy Bell. As on Wall Street, I punctuated this team's commencement of trading by ringing the bell, as in Buddy Bell. Despite having only a handful of at-bats at DH, this Bell earned his spot on the team over another one (Albert Belle), based on Buddy's longevity and consistency, best embodied by his 2,514 career hits.

The General Manager

Brian Cashman – For the person responsible for negotiating player contracts, having the name Cashman sure seems apropos.

Chapter Ten
The All-Time Location Team

Overview

For a player to qualify for this team, the full pronunciation of his first or last name must represent a well-known place, based on one of the following categories of places:

- Country (*e.g.*, Paris)
- U.S. state (*e.g.*, Washington, Maine)
- Capital city or major city within a country or a U.S. state (*e.g.*, Austin, Cairo, Santiago, Florence)
- College/university town/city (*e.g.*, Ames, Durham)
- Tourist/resort destination (*e.g.*, Vail)
- Famous street (*e.g.*, Broadway)
- Place of historical significance (*e.g.*, Troy)
- Planet or moon (*e.g.*, Moon)

Fun Facts

- Four members of the Hall of Fame have location names: executive Happy Chandler (large city in Arizona), Sam Crawford (Texas home to former President George W. Bush), Reggie and Travis Jackson (capital of Mississippi). Hall of Famers excluded for not quite meeting the geographic criteria above are Ferguson (Missouri) Jenkins and Oscar Charleston (South Carolina).
- Shoeless Joe Jackson (capital of Mississippi) is the all-time location-named leader in batting average(.356), to go with a career on-base percentage of .423.

- Top 500 batting averages among players with location-centric names include Sam Crawford (.309), Gary Sheffield (large city in England, .292), Troy Tulowitzski (Troy was a historical city in ancient Greece, .292), Travis Jackson(.291), Jeff Kent (English college town, .290), Carl Crawford (.290), Wally Moon (.289) and Clyde Milan (.285). Notable omissions from this list based on not quite meeting this team's geographic criteria are Ginger Beaumont (Texas) and Mickey Vernon (New Jersey).
- Top all-time location-named ERA leaders include relief pitcher Greg Holland (2.42), starter Red Ames (2.63), Roy Patterson (2.75), Spud Chandler (2.84), Huston (Houston) Street (2.97) and Al Holland (2.97). Criteria-based exclusions are Lefty Tyler (Texas), Charlie Ferguson and Ferguson Jenkins (Missouri).
- Clyde Milan is the all-time location-named base stealer, with 495.
- Reggie Jackson (Mississippi) is the all-time location-named leader in home runs, with 563. The next-closest are Garry Sheffield (509) and Jeff Kent (377).
- Huston (Houston) Street is the career leader in saves (324), followed by Jose Mesa (Arizona, 321) and Jeff Montgomery (Alabama, 304).
- Bartolo Colon (Cologne), who is still active, is the all-time location-named leader in wins ([233]).

Thought Process on Team Selection

Starting with the Hall of Fame, I had right fielder Reggie Jackson and shortstop Travis Jackson to work with. Although not in the Hall of Fame (by technicality), I also had outfielder Shoeless Joe Jackson. I knew one of these Jacksons would make the team, but which one depended on available positions.

In addition to the Jacksons, I had Hall of Fame right fielder Sam Crawford. Utilizing Crawford in right field would eliminate Reggie Jackson from consideration and allow use of one of the other Jacksons for either shortstop or left field. Shoeless Joe, while primarily a left fielder, did play all outfield positions, so he provided additional flexibility assuming other worthy shortstop candidates.

Looking over potential shortstops, I had Troy Tulowitzki. If his career were to end as of this writing, Troy's statistics would compare favorably to Travis Jackson's. As such, I knew I had some flexibility in shortstop selection.

With Gary Sheffield available in right field or at DH, plus Jeff Kent and Ray Durham as potential second basemen, filling the middle infield and completing the outfield seemed like reasonable expectations for this team, but the challenge of identifying the best players remained.

The most obvious choice at catcher seemed to be Benito Santiago (Chile) but required confirmatory research.

No first basemen stood out at first glance (bummer that Gehrig is not a large city somewhere).

For starting pitchers, I focused on top ERA leaders and those who had won at least 100 games. With these criteria in mind, my short list of starters included Reggie Cleveland (105 wins),

Mark Portugal (109 wins), Spud Chandler (109 wins), Danny Jackson (112 wins), Red Ames (183 wins), Larry Jackson (194 wins), Bartolo Colon (233 wins) and Roy Patterson (2.75 ERA). Danny Jackson would not work unless I was prepared not to select any of the top positional players named Jackson.

For relief pitchers, I looked at those near the top in career saves, which included: Huston Street, Jose Mesa and Jeff Montgomery, as well as ERA leaders Greg and Al Holland.

Overall, the pool of available players (including some with a location-centric name but who did not meet my stricter team criteria) included:

Last Name	First Name	Given Name
Alba	Gibson	Gibson Alberto
Alburquerque	Al	Alberto Jose
Ames	Red	Leon Kessling
Ames	Steve	Steven C.
Appier	Kevin	Robert Kevin
Austin	Henry	Henry C.
Austin	Jimmy	James Philip
Austin	Rick	Rick Gerald
Austin	Jim	James Parker
Austin	Jeff	Jeffrey Wellington
Birmingham	Joe	Joseph Leo
Bolton	Cliff	William Clifton
Bolton	Tom	Thomas Edward
Bolton	Rod	Rodney Earl
Bolton	Cecil	Cecil Glenford
Boston	Daryl	Daryl Lamont
Brandenburg	Mark	Mark Clay

Last Name	First Name	Given Name
Branson	Jeff	Jeffery Glenn
Brazill	Frank	Frank Leo
Breckinridge	Bill	William Robertson
Bristol	Dave	James David
Brittain	Gus	August Schuster
Broadway	Lance	Lance Daniel
Broadway	Mike	Michael Allen
Buckingham	Fred	Frederick Bristol
Cairo	Miguel	Miguel Jesus
Cali	Carmen	Carmen Salvatore
Capri	Pat	Patrick Nicholas
Chandler	Spud	Spurgeon Ferdinand
Chandler	Ed	Edward Oliver
Chandler	Happy	Albert Benjamin
Charleston	Oscar	Oscar McKinley
Chatham	Buster	Charles Lorenzo
Cicero	Joe	Joseph John
Cleveland	Elmer	Elmer Ellsworth
Cleveland	Reggie	Reginald Leslie
Colon	Bartolo	Bartolo
Colon	Christian	Christian Anthony
Colon	Cris	Cristobal
Colon	Roman	Roman Benedicto
Compton	Mike	Michael Lynn
Compton	Jack	Harry Leroy
Compton	Clint	Robert Clinton
Davenport	Jim	James Houston
Davenport	Dave	David W.
Davenport	Lum	Joubert Lum
Davenport	Joe	Joseph Jonathan
Davenport	Claude	Claude Edwin

Last Name	First Name	Given Name
Decatur	Art	Arthur Rue
Delhi	Flame	Lee William
Durham	Ray	Ray
Durham	Leon	Leon
Durham	Bull	Louis Staub
Durham	Joe	Joseph Vann
Durham	Ed	Edward Fant
Durham	Don	Donald Gary
Durham	James	James Garfield
Eden	Charlie	Charles M.
Eden	Mike	Edward Michael
Fajardo	Hector	Hector
Florence	Paul	Paul Robert
Florence	Don	Donald Emery
France	Ossie	Osman Beverly
Gibralter	Steve	Stephan Benson
Gilroy	Henry	Henry Engard
Gilroy	John	John M.
Guiney	Ben	Benjamin Franklin
Hague	Bill	William L.
Hague	Joe	Joe Clarence
Hague	Matt	Matthew Donald
Hamburg	Charlie	Charles H.
Hartford	Bruce	Bruce Daniel
Heredia	Gil	Gilbert
Heredia	Felix	Felix
Heredia	Wilson	Wilson
Heredia	Ubaldo	Ubaldo Jose
Holland	Will	Willard A.
Holland	Al	Alfred Willis
Holland	Derek	Derek Lane

Last Name	First Name	Given Name
Holland	Greg	Gregory Scott
Holland	Mul	Howard Arthur
Holland	Dutch	Robert Clyde
Holland	Bill	William David
Hollands	Mario	Mario Eduardo Lemus
Houston	Tyler	Tyler Sam
Ireland	Tim	Timothy Neal Christopher
Irvine	Daryl	Daryl Keith
Jackson	Henry	Henry Everett
Jackson	Sam	Samuel
Jackson	Reggie	Reginald Martinez
Jackson	Michael	Michael Ray
Jackson	Grant	Grant Dwight
Jackson	Darrin	Darrin Jay
Jackson	Travis	Travis Calvin
Jackson	Danny	Danny Lynn
Jackson	Larry	Lawrence Curtis
Jackson	Shoeless Joe	Joseph Walker
Jackson	Edwin	Edwin
Jackson	Sonny	Roland Thomas
Jackson	Al	Alvin Neill
Jackson	Damian	Damian Jacques
Jackson	Randy	Ransom Joseph
Jackson	Ron	Ronnie Damien
Jackson	Roy Lee	Roy Lee
Jackson	Bo	Vincent Edward
Jackson	Chuck	Charles Leo
Jackson	Conor	Conor Sims
Jackson	Ron	Ronald Harris
Jackson	Lou	Louis Clarence
Jackson	Austin	Austin Jarriel

Last Name	First Name	Given Name
Jackson	Jim	James Benner
Jackson	Ryan	Ryan Dewitte
Jackson	Darrell	Darrell Preston
Jackson	Mike	Michael Warren
Jackson	Ryan	Ryan Christopher
Jackson	Zach	Zachary Thomas
Jackson	Brett	Brett Elliott
Jackson	Charlie	Charles Herbert
Jackson	George	George Christopher
Jackson	Bill	William Riley
Jackson	Steven	Steven Nash
Jackson	John	John Lewis
Jackson	Luke	Luke Ray
Jackson	Ken	Kenneth Bernard
Jackson	Jay	Randy
Jackson	Herbert	Herbert Benjamin
Jungels	Ken	Kenneth Peter
Kent	Ed	Edward C.
Kent	Jeff	Jeffrey Franklin
Kent	Maury	Maurice Allen
Kent	Steven	Steven Patrick
Lancaster	Les	Lester Wayne
Lansing	Mike	Michael Thomas
Lansing	Gene	Eugene Hewitt
Latham	Jumbo	George Warren
Latham	Arlie	Walter Arlington
Latham	Chris	Christopher Joseph
Latham	Bill	William Carol
Lawrence	Brian	Brian Michael
Lawrence	Brooks	Brooks Ulysses
Lawrence	Joe	Joseph Dudley

Last Name	First Name	Given Name
Lawrence	Bill	William Henry
Lawrence	Sean	Sean Christopher
Lawrence	Jim	James Ross
Lawrence	Bob	Robert Andrew
Leicester	Jon	Jonathan David
Lennox	Ed	James Edgar
Lima	Jose	Jose Desiderio Rodriguez
Livingston	Paddy	Patrick Joseph
Livingston	Mickey	Thompson Orville
Livingston	Bobby	Robert James
Lombard	George	George Paul
Macon	Max	Max Cullen
Madison	Art	Arthur M.
Madison	Scotti	Charles Scott
Madison	Dave	David Pledger
Madrid	Alex	Alexander
Madrid	Sal	Salvator
Main	Woody	Forrest Harry
Main	Alex	Miles Grant
Maine	John	John Kevin
Maine	Scott	Scott
Mars	Ed	Edward M.
Medina	Luis	Luis Main
Medina	Yoervis	Yoervis Jose
Medina	Rafael	Rafael Eduardo
Mesa	Jose	Jose Ramon Nova
Mesa	Melky	Melquisedec
Milan	Clyde	Jesse Clyde
Milan	Horace	Horace Robert
Monaco	Blas	Blas
Montgomery	Jeff	Jeffrey Thomas

Last Name	First Name	Given Name
Montgomery	Bob	Robert Edward
Montgomery	Steve	Steven Lewis
Montgomery	Ray	Raymond James
Montgomery	Monty	Monty Bryson
Montgomery	Al	Alvin Atlas
Montgomery	Mike	Michael Paul
Moon	Wally	Wallace Wade
Moon	Leo	Leo
Naples	Al	Aloysius Francis
Needham	Tom	Thomas Joseph
Newton	Doc	Eustace James
Oberlin	Frank	Frank Rufus
Ogden	Jack	John Mahlon
Ogden	Curly	Warren Harvey
Oran	Tom	Thomas
Orlando	Paulo	Paulo Roberto
Paris	Kelly	Kelly Jay
Parris	Steve	Steven Michael
Phoenix	Steve	Steven Robert
Poland	Hugh	Hugh Reid
Pompey	Dalton	Dalton Kenrick
Ponce	Carlos	Carlos Antonio
Portugal	Mark	Mark Steven
Raleigh	John	John Austin
Rhodes	Arthur	Arthur Lee
Rhodes	Gordon	John Gordon
Rhodes	Dusty	James Lamar
Rhodes	Tuffy	Karl Derrick
Rhodes	Charlie	Charles Anderson
Santiago	Benito	Benito
Santiago	Ramon	Ramon DeJesus

Last Name	First Name	Given Name
Santiago	Jose	Jose Rafael
Santiago	Jose	Jose Rafael
Santiago	Hector	Hector Felipe
Santiago	Jose	Jose Guillermo
Santo Domingo	Rafael	Rafael
Santorini	Al	Alan Joel
Scranton	Jim	James Dean
Selma	Dick	Richard Jay
Shannon	Dan	Daniel Webster
Shannon	Frank	John Francis
Shannon	Red	Maurice Joseph
Shannon	Mike	Thomas Michael
Shannon	Spike	William Porter
Shannon	Owen	Owen Dennis Ignatius
Shannon	Wally	Walter Charles
Shannon	Joe	Joseph Aloysius
Sharon	Dick	Richard Louis
Sheffield	Gary	Gary Antonian
Shelton	Chris	Christopher Bob
Shelton	Ben	Benjamin Davis
Shelton	Skeeter	Andrew Kemper
Shirley	Bob	Robert Charles
Shirley	Tex	Alvis Newman
Shirley	Bart	Barton Arvin
Shirley	Mule	Ernest Raeford
Shirley	Steve	Steven Brian
Southwick	Clyde	Clyde Aubra
Stowe	Hal	Harold Rudolph
Strasburg	Stephen	Stephen James
Stratton	Asa	Asa Evans
Stratton	Scott	Chilton Scott

Last Name	First Name	Given Name
Stratton	Ed	William Edward
Stratton	Monty	Monty Franklin Pierce
Suarez	Ken	Kenneth Raymond
Suarez	Eugenio	Eugenio Alejandro
Suarez	Luis	Luis Abelardo
Sucre	Jesus	Jesus Marcelo
Tappan	Walter	Walter Van Dorn
Telford	Anthony	Anthony Charles
Troy	Dasher	John Joseph
Troy	Bun	Robert Gustave
Trujillo	Mike	Michael Andrew
Trujillo	J. J.	John
Trumbull	Ed	Edward J.
Vail	Mike	Michael Lewis
Vail	Bob	Robert Garfield
Valencia	Danny	Daniel Paul
Valera	Julio	Julio Enrique
Valera	Yohanny	Yohanny
Vandenberg	Hy	Harold Harris
Ventura	Robin	Robin Mark
Ventura	Yordano	Yordano
Ventura	Vince	Vincent
Vernon	Mickey	James Barton
Vernon	Joe	Joseph Henry
Viau	Lee	Leon A.
Vinton	Bill	William Miller
Vorhees	Cy	Henry Bert
Warwick	Bill	Firman Newton
Washington	Claudell	Claudell
Washington	Ron	Ronald
Washington	U. L.	U. L.

Last Name	First Name	Given Name
Washington	George	Sloan Vernon
Washington	Herb	Herbert Lee
Washington	LaRue	LaRue
Washington	Rico	Enrico Aliceno
Waterbury	Steve	Steven Craig
Westlake	Wally	Waldon Thomas
Westlake	Jim	James Patrick
Weston	Mickey	Michael Lee
Weston	Al	Alfred John
Whistler	Lew	Lewis W.
Widner	Wild Bill	William Waterfield
Winchester	Scott	Scott Joseph
Windsor	Jason	Jason David
Winston	Hank	Henry Rudolph
Winston	Darrin	Darrin Alexander
Wohlford	Jim	James Eugene
Wortham	Rich	Richard Cooper
Worthington	Al	Allan Fulton
Worthington	Craig	Craig Richard
Worthington	Red	Robert Lee
Wyckoff	Weldon	John Weldon
York	Tom	Thomas Jefferson
York	Rudy	Rudolph Preston
York	Jim	James Harlan
York	Lefty	James Edward
York	Mike	Michael David
York	Tony	Tony Batton

The Final Team

The Pitching Staff

Starting Pitcher 1 – Spurgeon "Spud" Chandler (Arizona). Chandler finished his career with a 109-43 record and 2.84 ERA. His .717 winning percentage ranks him second all-time in Major League history. This winning city from Arizona got my nod for the top spot on the All-Time Location Team's starting staff..

Starting Pitcher 2 – Leon "Red" Ames (Iowa). Ames finished his career with a 183 – 167 record and a 2.63 ERA in almost 3,200 innings of work. His low ERA made this Midwest city my choice for the number 2 starter.

Starting Pitcher 3 – Bartolo Colon (Cologne, Germany). This still-active pitcher holds the distinction of having the most wins (233) of any location-named pitcher. Cologne is a 2,000-year-old city in Germany – and Bartolo may very well be close in age. The former Cy Young winner was my choice for the third starter.

Starting Pitcher 4 – Ray Patterson (New Jersey). Representing the third-largest city in New Jersey, Ray offered an 81-72 record and a stellar 2.75 ERA, so he was my choice as starter number four.

Starting Pitcher 5 – Mark Portugal. I selected Portugal over Cleveland, and who could blame me? While their career statistics are very similar, I chose Portugal based simply on his having a winning career mark (109-95) versus Cleveland's 105-106 record. Cleveland actually had the slightly better ERA (4.01

vs 4.03), but Portugal started more games. The kicker, I guess, was that I'd rather travel to Portugal than Cleveland.

Closer – Huston Street. Huston is kind of like two places in one. First, Houston is the largest city in Texas, and second, "Street" is, of course, a generic term for a road. Another active player, Huston currently boasts a [42-34] record with a [2.97] ERA. His [324] saves ranks him first all-time among location-named players, and his total saves should continue to increase.

The Outfield

Center Field – Clyde Milan (Italy). Milan got the nod over Fred Lynn (Massachusetts) simply because Lynn was not a large enough city (eighth-largest in Massachusetts) to qualify Lynn for this team. Still, Milan had a great career, with 2,100 hits, 495 stolen bases, a .285 batting average and a .353 on-base percentage.

Right Field – Sam Crawford (Texas). This Hall of Famer made the team over fellow Hall of Famer Reggie Jackson. Crawford finished his career with 2,961 hits, 366 stolen bases, a .309 batting average and a .362 on-base percentage.

Left Field – Joe Jackson (Mississippi). I chose Shoeless Joe over Reggie and Travis of the same surname. Joe's career batting average of .356 and on-base percentage of .423 rank him third and 14th all-time, respectively, and, of course, first all-time for a location-named player.

The Infield and Designated Hitter

Catcher – Benito Santiago (Chile). Santiago was an easy choice as catcher. He was a three-time Gold Glove winner, five-time All-Star and four-time Silver Slugger winner. He finished his career with 1,830 hits, 217 home runs, a .263 batting average and a .307 on-base percentage.

First Base – Rudy York (England). York made the team over Mickey Vernon (New Jersey), since Vernon is just a township. York finished his career with 1,621 hits (well short of the 2,495 by Vernon), 277 home runs, a .275 batting average and a .362 on-base percentage.

Second Base – Jeff Kent (England). Kent is another England location represented on the team. Jeff is the Major League career leader in home runs by a second baseman. He finished his career with 2,461 hits, 377 home runs, a .290 batting average and a .356 on-base percentage.

Shortstop – Troy Tulowitski (ancient Greece and present-day New York). Troy is another active player who made the team. He currently has a career [.292] batting average, [.364] on-base percentage. [217] home runs and [1,329] hits. While injuries have slowed him down, I expect him eventually to enter the Hall of Fame.

Third Base – Jim Davenport (Iowa). Another Iowa location made the team here – and once again over a more worthy player (this time, Robin Ventura, California) who has the misfortune of not being a big enough city in its state. Davenport is the fourth largest city in Iowa. Jim finished his career with 1,142 hits, a

.258 batting average and a .318 on-base percentage. He was a two-time All-Star and won one Gold Glove award.

Designated Hitter – Gary Sheffield (England). Sheffield was yet another English location to make the team. While primarily a right fielder that came up to the Majors as an infielder, Sheffield luckily spent time at DH as well. Overall, he amassed 509 career home runs, 2,689 hits, a .292 batting average and a .393 on-base percentage.

Chapter Eleven
The All-Time Smith Team

Overview

Since Smith is such a common surname in the U.S., I decided to create a theme team consisting solely of players with the last name of Smith. Sorry, no Smithes, Smythes, Messersmiths or Goldsmiths are permitted on the roster.

Fun Facts

- Smith is the most common name among all players to in Major League history, with over 140 active and former Smiths (next in popularity are Johnson and Jones).
- Two Smiths are in the Hall of Fame, Negro League standout pitcher Hilton Smith (inducted in 2001) and shortstop Ozzie Smith (2002).
- Four Smiths rank in the top 500 of all-time batting average leaders. They are, in order: Elmer Elsworth Smith (.310), Lonnie (.288), Reggie (.287) and Jack (.287).
- Four Smiths also rank in the top 500 career ERA leaders: Frank (2.59), Dave (2.67), Charlie (2.81) and Lee (3.03).
- Two Smiths rank in the top 50 of all-time saves leaders. Lee Smith is ranked third all-time, with 478 saves, and Dave is ranked 37th, with 216. In fact, Lee was the all-time saves leader until recently surpassed by Trevor Hoffman and Mariano Rivera.
- The most common nickname for a Smith was "Red," four of whom have played in the Majors.

- The best nickname of any Smith arguably belongs to John Francis Smith, whose nickname was "Phenomenal," although his statistics suggest that he was anything but that. He finished his career with a 54 – 74 record. In 1887, he won 25 games. Unfortunately, he lost 30 in the same year. pitching 491 innings. I guess pitch counts were a bit higher back then!
- The most career wins for a Smith belongs to Frank, with 139.
- Reggie Smith holds the record for most home runs by a Smith, with 314.
- The record for most stolen bases by a Smith belongs to Ozzie, with 580, leaving him 21st on the all-time leaders list.
- As you'll see below, the St. Louis Cardinals are well represented on the All-Time Smith Team. A majority (seven) of its members played with the Cardinals.
- The Braves of Boston and Atlanta are also represented, with five players on the team having spent some time in a Braves uniform.

Thought Process on Team Selection

Overall team selection was easy in this case, because the pool of players was clearly identifiable and limited to the approximately 140 Smiths to have played the game. Several of the Smiths played all of their careers before 1900, so I decided to eliminate these players and focus instead on those who played at least a majority of their careers post 1900.

The steepest challenge was finding the best Smiths for each given position, especially since some positions, such as second base, offered very little talent.

In general, the name Smith was well represented, but its representatives did not particularly stand out based on statistical qualifications. The obvious lock for the team was Hall of Fame shortstop Ozzie. Negro League standout and fellow Hall of Famer Hilton Smith also deserved recognition.

Selecting the remaining players came down to a relatively small pool of players, many of whom spent fewer than three years in the Major Leagues.

Since I didn't need to worry about replication of names for this team, the final selection came down to identifying the best Smith by position. The primary offensive statistics I reviewed were batting average, on-base percentage, slugging percentage, OPS (on-base percentage + slugging percentage), stolen bases and home runs. For pitchers, I looked at wins, winning percentage, ERA, strikeouts, batting average against and the number of top-25 all-time career rankings.

For this team, I did not select a designated hitter.

<u>The Final Team</u>

The Pitching Staff

Starting Pitcher 1 – Hilton Smith. The top spot as ace of the All-Time Smith Team belongs to the only Hall of Fame Smith pitcher, Hilton Smith. The official negro league statistics list

Hilton's career record at 71 – 31. Even more impressive than his nearly .700 winning percentage is his 1.68 ERA.

Starting Pitcher 2 – Frank Smith. Frank slots in as the number 2 pitcher of this staff. Frank has the best lifetime ERA (2.59) of all Smiths who played in the Majors and the most career wins of any Smith (139). Pitching most of his career for the Chicago White Sox, he recorded his best year in 1909, posting a 25 – 17 record with a 1.80 ERA. Interestingly enough, his 1.80 ERA was only eighth-best in the American League that year, although he did lead the league that year in strikeouts (177) and innings pitched (365).

Starting Pitcher 3 – Bryn Smith. Bryn finished his career with a 108 – 94 record. Bryn distinguished himself as the only Smith (other than Frank) with a winning record and at least 100 victories. Bryn is one of several all-time Smiths to have played part of his career for the Cardinals.

Starting Pitcher 4 – Bob Smith. The last two starters were the most difficult to select, from a pool of six starters (and pitchers who were primarily starters) with very similar statistics. It came down to Zane, Charlie, Sherry, Eddie, Bob and Al. The fact that these players came from different eras further complicated comparisons among them. Bob got the nod in the end because he had more top-25 finishes in innings pitched, wins, games started, ERA, strikeouts and batting average against than any of the other candidates. His versatility as a relief pitcher also enhanced his standing, as he finished in the top 25 in saves 11 times in his career (although saves were not as common in his era), which helped to offset his unremarkable 106 – 139 win/loss record. Bob is one of several Smiths to have played for the Braves.

Starting Pitcher 5 – Sherry Smith. Sherry finished his career at 114 – 118 and a 3.32 ERA. He was the toughest pitcher to select. He has the second-most wins of any Smith. He got the nod in a very tight contest over two-time All-Star Eddie and one-time All-Stars Al and Zane. What sealed it for me was that Sherry had the best winning percentage early in his career and was still an above-.500 pitcher until his last three years in the Majors.

Closer – Lee Smith. At first, I thought this was an easy selection. However, when reviewing Dave Smith's statistics, it became not quite the same slam-dunk selection as, say, shortstop. Dave had the superior ERA (2.67 vs. 3.03). However, Lee's longevity and total body of work simplified my choice. Lee is ranked third all-time in saves and helped to reinvent the closer position. He was a seven-time All-Star with four different teams, including three selections while with the Cardinals.

The Outfield

Center Field – Lonnie Smith. Lonnie was a solid all-around player. His lifetime .288 batting average, .371 on-base percentage and 370 career stolen bases all rank him in the top 500 of all-time in those respective categories. The Cardinals and Braves (Atlanta) are two of the teams for which Lonnie played during his career.

Right Field – Jack Smith. Jack had similar statistics to Lonnie, albeit with a lower on-base percentage. Jack played both center field and right field, primarily with the St. Louis Cardinals. He finished with a .287 career batting average and a .339 on-base percentage. In addition to the Cardinals, Jack played with the Boston Braves.

Left Field – Elmer John Smith. There are two Elmer Smiths who played in the outfield. The statistically better Smith (Elmer Ellsworth) played before the turn of the 20th century, however, so he was excluded from consideration for this team. Elmer John played a majority of his career with the Cleveland Indians. Although he was primarily a right fielder, he could and did play all three outfield positions over his career. His .276 batting average and .344 on-base percentage made him a worthy selection.

The Infield

Catcher – Earl Smith. Although he never caught more than 109 games in any year, Earl put up some very impressive statistics. In 2,264 career at-bats over an 11-year period, Earl finished with 686 hits and a lifetime .303 batting average, playing for the New York Giants, Pittsburgh Pirates and St. Louis Cardinals. He also had a lifetime .374 on-base percentage and .806 OPS.

First Base – Reggie Smith. The all-time Smith homerun king, Reggie was a lock to make this team. In addition to his 314 home runs, Reggie was a seven-time All-Star with a lifetime .287 batting average,.366 on-base percentage and.855 OPS. Reggie played a majority of his career with the Red Sox, but, like many members of the all-Smith team, he also played at one time for the Cardinals.

Second Base – James (Jimmy) Smith. This is the weakest position for the All-Time Smith team. Jimmy is one of seven Smiths whose primary position was second base, two of whom played prior to 1900. Jimmy, who played from 1914 to 1922, got the nod over Pop Smith, who amassed considerably more hits – but all of them prior to 1900. Jimmy finished his career with just 247 hits and a .219 batting average. He is one of many on the All-Time Smith Team to have played for the Braves.

Shortstop – Ozzie Smith. This was the easiest position to fill. The Wizard of Oz is a Hall of Fame shortstop and the best Smith to have played the game. His 2,460 hits easily make him the Smith hit king. Ozzie played a majority of his career with the Cardinals.

Third Base – Red Smith. James "Red" Smith, one of the four Smiths who went by "Red," played for the Brooklyn Dodgers and Boston Braves. He amassed 1,087 hits in a career that spanned from 1911 to 1919. He had a career .278 batting average and .353 on-base percentage.

Chapter Twelve
The All-Time Jones Team

Overview

I figured if I was going to have an all-Smith team, then I had to assemble an all-Jones team as well. After all, Jones is another popular U.S. surname. However, there are fewer Joneses than Smiths to have played in the Majors.

To be included on this team, the player's last name has to be Jones.

For this team, I did not select a designated hitter.

Fun Facts

- Jones is the third-most popular surname in Major League history, behind Smith and Johnson. Ninety-five Joneses have played in the Major Leagues, more than 50 fewer than the number of Smiths.
- There is currently no Jones in the Hall of Fame.
- Three players named Bobby Jones have played in the Major Leagues. In fact, in 2000, the Mets featured two players named Bobby Jones on their team (Bobby M and Bobby J). In the same year, the Braves also had two Joneses, although they did not share the same first name (Larry, aka Chipper, and Andruw).
- Chipper Jones is the all-time career batting average leader among Joneses, with a .303 average.
- Oscar Jones is the only Jones in the top 500 career ERA leaders, although he only pitched in 113 games.

- Randy Jones was the first – and to this day is the only – Jones ever to win the Cy Young Award.
- Chipper and Andruw are first and second, respectively, on the career Jones home run list. Chipper had 468 and Andruw had 434. Next closest is Willie, with 190.
- Fielder Jones is the all-time Jones stolen base leader, with 359.
- Sad Sam Jones is the all-time Jones win leader, with 229.
- No Jones whose primary position was catcher ever has played in the Major Leagues. Only one game post 1900 included a catcher by the name of Jones, and that was Tim Jones, whose primary position was shortstop.
- All Joneses have combined for fewer than 300 games played at shortstop. Tim Jones recorded the most games at shortstop by a Jones, with 119, followed by Chipper Jones, with 49. Collectively, Tim and Chipper played in more than 50% of all games played by a shortstop named Jones.
- Dalton Jones holds the record for most games played at second base by a Jones, with 267.

Thought Process on Team Selection

With only 95 Joneses to choose from, the team was bound to have some holes. The most glaring holes were at catcher, shortstop and second base. No primary catchers named Jones have played in the Major Leagues. In fact, in baseball history, only eight games in total have been played at catcher by someone named Jones. Further, only 296 total games in baseball history have been played at shortstop by someone named Jones.

And only 477 combined games have been played at second base by someone named Jones, of which more than half (267) were played by Dalton Jones, whose primary position was third base. After removing games played prior to 1900 from consideration, the number of total games played at catcher, shortstop and second base drops to one, 244 and 429, respectively.

In light of the above, sticking with a post-1900 roster made catcher an easy choice, as the only game played by a catcher named Jones after 1900 dictated the selection.

To fill the rest of the team, I decided to focus on the best players at their primary positions, knowing that there would be holes at shortstop and second base. I figured once I had the best position players, I could then be creative and use secondary or tertiary player positions to fill the middle infield.

For example, I felt fairly confident that Chipper Jones was going to be the all-Jones third baseman over Willie Jones. Chipper is both the all-time Jones home run and average leader, but he also played some games at shortstop and left field. Since the vast majority of his games were at third base, though, I thought I had to stick with him as a third baseman. Since Chipper's selection eliminated Willie Jones from third base (Willie played over 1,600 games there and is second only to Chipper in games played at third base by someone named Jones), I intended to circle back to see for which, if any, other positions Willie might qualify within the infield.

The bottom line was that to fill this team, some creative positioning was going to be necessary to fill out the middle infield positions.

Outfield was a bit more straightforward. There was an adequate supply of outfield talent to select from, although no single outfielder stood out from the pool (which included Andruw, Fielder, Ruppert, Cleon, Davy and Jacque).

Pitching was a bit like the outfield, as there were several pitchers to choose from with similar lifetime statistics.

The Final Team

The Pitching Staff

Starting Pitcher 1 – Sam Pond Jones. Sam is the all-time winningest pitcher for someone named Jones. Over his 20-plus year career, he amassed 229 wins playing for the Indians, Red Sox, Yankees, Senators and White Sox. His best year was in 1923 for the New York Yankees. Sam finished with a 21 – 8 record, which was second best in the American League.

Starting Pitcher 2 – Sam "Toothpick Sam" Jones. The other Sam Jones finished his career above .500, with a 102-101 record. Toothpick Sam led the league in strikeouts three times, in wins and ERA once each and in batting average against twice.

Starting Pitcher 3 – Randy Jones. Although he finished his career with a sub-.500 record (100 – 123), his career ERA of 3.42 is tops among starting pitchers named Jones with a minimum of 1,000 innings pitched.

Starting Pitcher 4 – Bobby J Jones. Bobby J makes the team because he had a career winning percentage above .500 (89 –

83). Bobby J pitched a majority of his career with the New York Mets, compiling a 74 – 56 record (a .569 winning percentage).

Starting Pitcher 5 – Sheldon Jones got the nod over Jimmy and Percy. Sheldon, Jimmy and Percy had very comparable won/loss records (Sheldon, 54 – 57; Jimmy, 43 – 39; Percy, 53 – 57). Sheldon led in career ERA, at 3.96, versus 4.46 for Jimmy and 4.34 for Percy. Although Jimmy had the only winning record among them, I felt ERA was a better judge of performance.

Closer – Doug Jones. Doug got the role of closer over Todd. Doug is second to Todd in all-time saves by a Jones (303 versus 319). Doug and Todd have similar innings pitched and total strikeouts statistics. However, Doug was far superior in ERA (3.30 vs. 3.97) and WHIP (1.24 vs 1.41). Doug is the career ERA leader for someone named Jones with a minimum of 1,000 innings pitched, which clinched his spot for the closer role.

The Outfield

Center Field – Andruw Jones. No other Jones has played more games in center field than Andruw. The next-closest was Ruppert Jones, but Andruw got the nod for his power and defense. Andruw ranks third all-time for hits by a Jones.

Right Field – Fielder Jones. With a name of Fielder, you would expect this Jones to play a great right field. Fielder is second all-time for hits by a Jones, with 1,920. Fielder finished his career with a .285 batting average and .368 on-base percentage. His 359 stolen bases rank him as the number one base stealer for a Jones.

Left Field – Cleon Jones. Cleon won out over Ruppert, Davy and Jacque Jones. Cleon was primarily a left fielder, which set him apart from the other Joneses. He played more games in left field than any other Jones and finished his career with a respectable .281 batting average, .339 on-base percentage and .744 OPS.

The Infield

Catcher – William Timothy ("Tim") Jones. Tim has the distinction of being the only person named Jones to catch a game in the Major Leagues post 1900. This and only this distinction land this career .233 hitter as the starting catcher on the All-Time Jones Team. This is one position begging for a replacement.

First Base – Thomas Jones. A lifetime .251 hitter with a .294 on-base percentage and .597 OPS is hardly the stuff of all-stars. However, his 964 career hits are almost 500 more than the next-closest Jones who played first base (Nippy). I also gave some edge to Thomas for having played during the dead ball era.

Second Base – Willie "Puddin Head" Jones. Willie was primarily a third baseman, but he did play one game at second base, recording one put-out. Ignoring games played at second base by Tom and Tim (who already have been slotted at first base and catcher on the All-Time Jones Team, per above), only 327 games since 1900 have been played at second base by a Jones. So, Willie played in 0.3% of all games played at second base by a Jones. Of the remaining candidates, his one game ranks him tied for sixth all-time in games played at second base by a Jones. Dalton, another primary third baseman, was the leader in games played at second base by a Jones (262) but finished his career with a .235 batting average and .295 on-base percentage. Willie's career .258 batting average and .343 on-base percentage were superior enough to Dalton's to justify Willie's selection to this team.

Shortstop – Robert ("Bob") Ducky Jones. Bob was another third baseman that made the team out of position, due to a lack of available alternatives. He qualifies by having played in one game at shortstop in 1920. Absent Tim and Chipper's games played at shortstop, only 76 games since 1900 have been played at shortstop by a Jones. To put it in perspective, Bob has played in 1.3% of all games played at shortstop by a Jones, which is substantial enough to make this team. Even so, Bob's lifetime .265 average, .314 on-base percentage and .651 OPS would be unlikely to stand out for consideration on any other all-time team.

Third Base – Lawrence "Chipper" Jones. Chipper stands alone as the best player named Jones. He ranks first in batting average ([.307]), home runs ([426]), on-base percentage ([.406]) and OPS ([.944]). Add in his 144 stolen bases and versatility (having played both shortstop and left field), and this is one deserving member of the All-Time Jones team.

Chapter Thirteen
The All-Time Gonzalez/Martinez Team

Overview

In the 1950s, Latin/Hispanic players represented less than 4% of all Major Leaguers. In 2017[?], according to statistics compiled by Major League Baseball, [27]% of current Major Leaguers are considered Latin/Hispanic.

With such a large percentage of players of Latin/Hispanic descent, an all-time team devoted to the more popular Latin/Hispanic surnames was in order. Since a majority of Latin/Hispanic players played post 1950, there is a relatively small historical pool to select from, so I expanded the team to include two popular Latin/Hispanic surnames: Gonzalez and Martinez.

For a player to qualify for this team, his last name must be either Gonzalez or Martinez.

Since a majority of the eligible players are from more recent times, I included a designated hitter on this team.

Fun Facts
- A total of 82 Martinezes and Gonzalezes have played in the Major Leagues (44 and 38, respectively).
- Juan Gonzalez leads all Gonzalezes with 434 home runs. Tino Martinez leads all Martinezes with 339 home runs.

- Edgar Martinez leads all Martinezes and Gonzalezes with a lifetime batting average of .312 and on-base percentage of .418.
- Luis Gonzalez leads all Martinezes and Gonzalezes in hits, with a total of 2,591.
- Gonzalezes and Martinezes seem to shy away from third base. There have been only two full-time third basemen (Denny Gonzalez and Edgar Martinez), although injuries limited Edgar to primarily a DH role. Two others have had put-outs from third base – Pedro and Marwin Gonzalez.
- Shortstop is the most common position (other than pitcher) for those with the last name of Martinez or Gonzalez.
- There have been two shortstops named Alex Gonzalez. Their careers overlapped, and their statistics are eerily similar.
- Dennis Martinez leads all Martinezes and Gonzalezes in career wins, with 245.
- Pedro Martinez leads all Martinezes and Gonzalezes in ERA, with a career 2.93 mark.

Thought Process on Team Selection

A small pool of players (here, 82) is much more manageable to work with. The first step in selecting this team was to weed out as many players as possible, first by filtering out players with fewer than five years of MLB service time. This restriction immediately eliminated 45 of the 82 players.

With a remaining list of only 37 players, sorting by primary position yielded a workable list but also surfaced a possible need to expand the list a bit, given the presence of only one full-time third baseman and second baseman (Denny Gonzalez and Fernando Gonzalez, respectively).

First base offered Adrian Gonzalez and Tino Martinez to choose from.

At catcher, there were Buck Martinez, Mike Gonzalez and Victor Martinez, who also could serve as DH.

The two Alex Gonzalezes and Ramon Martinez seemed to be the most likely shortstop candidates but it was also worth confirming whether either played any significant time at other positions.

At pitcher, Dennis and Pedro Martinez were two obvious choices, but finding the others required a closer examination.

<u>The Final Team</u>

The Pitching Staff

Starting Pitcher 1 – Pedro Martinez. Pedro was arguably the most dominant pitcher of his era. His career winning percentage of .687 (219 – 100) is sixth-best in MLB history.

Starting Pitcher 2 – Dennis Martinez. With 245 career wins, the most by a pitcher named Martinez or Gonzalez, Dennis was the clear choice as the #2 starter for this team.

Starting Pitcher 3 – Pedro's older brother Ramon finished his career with a record of 135-88 and an ERA of 3.67.

Starting Pitcher 4 – Gio Gonzalez. A currently active player, Gio has over 100 career wins ([102-77]) and a [3.72] ERA.

Starting Pitcher 5 – Carlos E. Martinez. Another currently active pitcher, this selection for the fifth starter spot was the toughest choice to make. Primarily used as a starter by the St. Louis Cardinals, Carlos has compiled a [34-21] record with a [3.32] ERA. Carlos got the nod over more experienced pitchers Geremi Gonzalez (nine-year career with 30 total wins) and Edgar Gonzalez (nine-year career with 17 total wins).

Closer – Tippy Martinez. Tippy is the career saves leader among Gonzalezes and Martinezes. He finished his career with a 55 - 42 record, a 3.45 ERA and 115 saves.

The Outfield

Center Field – Andres Antonio (Tony) Gonzalez. Tony played the bulk of his career with the Phillies, finishing second in the National League batting race in 1967, with a .339 average. Tony finished his career with 1,485 hits, a .286 batting average, a .350 on-base percentage and 143 home runs.

Right Field – Juan Gonzalez. Juan spent the prime of his career as a feared hitter for the Texas Rangers, finishing with 434 home runs, a .295 batting average and a .343 on-base percentage. Juan was the American League MVP in 1996 and 1998.

Left Field – Luis Gonzalez. Luis is the all-time Gonzalez/Martinez leader in hits, with 2,591. He finished his career with 354 home runs, a .283 batting average and a .367 on-base percentage.

The Infield and Designated Hitter

Catcher – Victor Martinez. Although used later in his career as a DH and first baseman, Victor came up to the Major Leagues as a catcher. With [1,936] hits and counting and a career batting average and on-base percentage currently at [.301] and [.366], respectively, Victor is clearly one of the best overall Martinez/Gonzalez hitters of all-time.

First Base – Adrian Gonzalez. Adrian is an active player who got the nod over Tino Martinez. This is one instance where an active player received preferential consideration over a retired player with similar statistics. Tino leads Adrian in home runs (339 –[308]). However, Adrian has more hits ([1,954] to 1,925) and will only further outpace Tino as Adrian's career winds down. Adrian also currently leads in batting average ([.290] to .271) and on-base percentage ([.362] to .344).

Second Base – Luis Alberto Gonzalez. This team's second Luis Gonzalez was sort of a wild card selection. For second base, I opted here for quality over longevity. This Luis only played for two seasons. However, he did finish his career with 248 hits, 23 home runs, a .283 batting average and a .321 on-base percentage. With few alternatives to choose from, Luis' relatively high batting average made him the choice.

Shortstop – Alex Gonzalez (but which one?). This Alex Gonzalez started his MLB career in 1998 with the Florida Marlins (the other Alex started his career in 1994 with Toronto). This team's selected Alex had 1,418 career hits and 157 career home runs (versus 1,209 and 137). The anointed Alex edged the other Alex in batting average (.245 to .243) but came up short in on-base percentage (.290 to .302). The 200 additional hits tilted my selection to the Marlins' Alex over Toronto's.

Third Base – Denny Gonzalez. Despite only 54 career hits, Denny made the team since no other third baseman was available to fill the spot.

Designated Hitter – Edgar Martinez. Edgar was one of the best hitters of all-time, as evidenced by his career .312 batting average and top-20 all-time on-base percentage of .418. I was tempted to slot Edgar at third base and use Tino Martinez as the DH but felt that his limited time at third base and debilitating knee injury disqualified him from being positioned there.

Chapter Fourteen
The All-Time Weather Team

<u>Overview</u>

From rain (Steve Rain) to sleet (Lou Sleater) to snow (J.T. Snow), this team consists of players with weather-related names. The list of weather terms (taken from TimeandDate.com) used to determine player eligibility is as follows:

Arctic	Confluence	Evening	Hygrometer	Normal	Spring
Autumn	Congestus	Fahrenheit	Ice	Offshore	Steam
Barometer	Convection	Fair	Inclement	Onshore	Storm
Beach	Convergence	Flood	Insolation	Outflow	Summer
Blizzard	Cumulus	Flurry	Instability	Overcast	Sunny
Blowing	Cyclone	Fog	Intermittent	Overrunning	Temperature
Blustery	Day	Forecast	Inversion	Ozone	Thunder
Breezy	Depression	Freeze	Iridescence	Polar	Tornado
Bright	Dew	Front	Katabatic	Precipitation	Tropical
Brisk	Difluence	Frost	Katafront	Pressure	Trough
Calm	Disturbance	Gale	Leeward	Radar	Twister
Celsius	Downburst	Greenhouse	Lifting	Rain	Typhoon
Chinook	Downdraft	Gust	Lightning	Rainbow	Warm
Cirrus	Draft	Hail	Low	Sandstorm	Wave
Clear	Drift	Haze	Melt	Saturation	Westerly
Clement	Drizzle	Heat	Mild	Shower	Weather
Climate	Drought	High	Mist	Sleet	Wind
Cloud(y)	Dry	Hot	Monsoon	Smog	Winter
Cold	Easterly	Humidity	Morning	Snow	Zonal
Condensation	Evaporation	Hurricane	Muggy	Spray	

The key to eligibility is that the pronunciation of the player's name must match a term (or form of the term) from the above list. For example, Dewey matches "Dew" and Freese matches "Freeze" but Blowers (rhymes with "ours") does not match "Blow."

Fun Facts
- There are over 125 players with weather-related names, including several who played prior to 1900.
- Two Hall of Famers had weather-related names: Roberto Clemente (clement) and Don Drysdale (dry or dries).
- Roberto Clemente leads all weather players with 3,000 career hits and a .317 batting average. Sammy Hale is the only other weather player with at least 1,000 at bats to have a career average over .300.
- Tim Raines Sr. leads all weather related players with 808 stolen bases.

Thought Process on Team Selection

The initial pool of weather candidates includes the following players:

Last	First	Given	Term
Albright	Jack	Harold John	Bright
Beach	Jack	Stonewall Jackson	Beach
Beachy	Brandon	Brandon Alan	Beach
Below	Duane	Duane Arthur	Below
Bright	Harry	Harry James	Bright
Calmus	Dick	Richard Lee	Calm
Childers	Jason	Jason Lee	Chill

Last	First	Given	Term
Childers	Matt	Matthew Wilkie	Chill
Childers	Bill	William	Chill
Childress	Rocky	Rodney Osborne	Chill
Clear	Mark	Mark Alan	Clear
Cleary	Joe	Joseph Christopher	Clear
Clement	Fred	Frederick Garwood	Clement
Clement	Jeff	Jeffrey Burton	Clement
Clement	Matt	Matthew Paul	Clement
Clement	Wally	Wallace Oakes	Clement
Clemente	Edgard	Edgard Alexis Velazquez	Clement
Clemente	Roberto	Roberto	Clement
Clements	Jack	John J.	Clement
Clements	Pat	Patrick Brian	Clement
Cloude	Ken	Kenneth Brian	Cloud
Coolbaugh	Mike	Michael Robert	Cool
Coolbaugh	Scott	Scott Robert	Cool
Cooley	Duff	Duff Gordon	Cool
Day	Dewon	Amos Dewon	Day
Day	Boots	Charles Frederick	Day
Day	Pea Ridge	Henry Clyde	Day
Day	John	John B.	Day
Day	Leon	Leon	Day
Day	Zach	Stephen Zachary	Day
Day	Bill	William J.	Day
Dayett	Brian	Brian Kelly	Day
Dayley	Ken	Kenneth Grant	Day
Dewey	Mark	Mark Alan	Dew
Drissel	Mike	Michael F.	Drizzle
Druhot	Carl	Carl A.	Hot
Drysdale	Don	Donald Scott	Dry

Last	First	Given	Term
Easterly	Jamie	James Morris	Easterly
Easterly	Ted	Theodore Harrison	Easterly
Ebright	Hi	Hiram C.	Bright
Flood	Curt	Curtis Charles	Flood
Flood	Tim	Timothy Andrew	Flood
Fogarty	Jim	James G.	Fog
Fogarty	John	John J.	Fog
Fogel	Horace	Horace S.	Fog
Fogg	Josh	Joshua Smith	Fogg
Freese	David	David Richard	Freeze
Freese	Gene	Eugene Lewis	Freeze
Freese	George	George Walter	Freeze
Freeze	Jake	Carl Alexander	Freeze
Frost	Dave	Carl David	Frost
Gale	Rich	Richard Blackwell	Gale
Gale	Rocky	Rocky Michael	Gale
Galehouse	Denny	Dennis Ward	Gale
Galle	Stan	Stanley Joseph	Gale
Gust	Ernie	Ernest Herman Frank	Gust
Hale	Odell	Arvel Odell	Hail
Hale	David	David E.	Hail
Hale	George	George Wagner	Hail
Hale	John	John Steven	Hail
Hale	Dad	Ray Luther	Hail
Hale	Bob	Robert Houston	Hail
Hale	Sammy	Samuel Douglas	Hail
Hale	Chip	Walter William	Hail
Haley	James	James	Hail
Haley	Raymond	Raymond Timothy	Hail
Hazewood	Drungo	Drungo LaRue	Haze
Heaton	Neal	Neal	Heat

Last	First	Given	Term
High	Andy	Andrew Aird	High
High	Charlie	Charles Edwin	High
High	Ed	Edward Thomas	High
High	Hugh	Hugh Jenkin	High
Hottman	Ken	Kenneth Roger	Hot
Hoyt	LaMarr	Dewey LaMarr	Dew
Low	Fletcher	Fletcher	Low
Lowe	Charlie	Charles	Low
Lowe	Derek	Derek Christopher	Low
Lowe	George	George Wesley	Low
Lowe	Sean	Jonathan Sean	Low
Lowe	Mark	Mark Christopher	Low
Lowe	Dick	Richard Alvern	Low
Lowe	Bobby	Robert Lincoln	Low
MacLeod	Billy	William Daniel	Cloud
McHale	Jim	James Bernard	Hail
McHale	John	John Joseph	Hail
McHale	Marty	Martin Joseph	Hail
McHale	Bob	Robert Emmet	Hail
McLeod	Ralph	Ralph Alton	Cloud
McLeod	Jim	Soule James	Cloud
Melter	Steve	Stephen Blasius	Melt
Merewether	Art	Arthur Francis	Weather
Rain	Steve	Steven Nicholas	Rain
Raines	Larry	Lawrence Glenn Hope	Rain
Raines	Tim	Timothy	Rain
Raines	Tim	Timothy	Rain
Rainey	Chuck	Charles David	Rain
Rainey	John	John M.	Rain
Raney	Ribs	Frank Robert Donald	Rain
Robinson	Dewey	Dewey Everett	Dew

Last	First	Given	Term
Rumbelow	Nick	Nicholas Bruno	Below
Shines	Razor	Anthony Razor	Shine
Snopek	Chris	Christopher Charles	Snow
Snow	Charlie	Charles M.	Snow
Snow	J. T.	Jack Thomas	Snow
Somerville	Ed	Edward G.	Summer
Spring	Jack	Jack Russell	Spring
Springer	Brad	Bradford Louis	Spring
Springer	Dennis	Dennis LeRoy	Spring
Springer	Ed	Edward Ellsworth	Spring
Springer	George	George Chelston	Spring
Springer	Russ	Russell Paul	Spring
Springer	Steve	Steven Michael	Spring
Summers	Champ	John Junior	Summer
Summers	Ed	Oren Edgar	Summer
Summers	Kid	William	Summer
Warmoth	Cy	Wallace Walter	Warm
Weatherly	Roy	Cyril Roy	Weather
Weathers	David	John David	Weather
Wetherby	Jeff	Jeffrey Barret	Weather
Williams	Dewey	Dewey Edgar	Dew
Windhorn	Gordie	Gordon Ray	Wind
Winter	George	George Lovington	Winter
Winters	Clarence	Clarence John	Winter
Winters	Jesse	Jesse Frank	Winter
Winters	Matt	Matthew Littleton	Winter

Starting with the Hall of Fame netted me a right fielder (and mild weather) in Roberto Clement(e) and a Don Dry(sdale) day.

Looking at top hitters of all-time, I found that Tim Raines Sr. (LF), Odell Hale (2B), Sammy Hale (3B), Curt Flood (CF) and Andy High (3B) were the potential top position players for this weather team.

George Winter and his career 2.87 ERA also made a short list of pitching candidates.

Filtering the pool of players down to those with at least six years of MLB experience and who played all or most of their careers after 1900 reduced the pool of candidates to a manageable list of 39, with only one catcher (which made that position easy to fill). The big issue was that the resulting list of 39 included no shortstops, so I was going to need to see if any of the other infielders played some time at short and, if so, how that might impact other positions.

First base candidates included Harry Bright, J.T. Snow and Bob Hale. There were several Hales available, I had to give thought to which Hale made the most sense to select, based on position.

At second base, my options were Odell Hale, Chip Hale and Bobby all-time Lowe. Derek Lowe was an option at pitcher, so selecting Bobby Lowe at second base would have an impact there.

At third base, I had to choose from Hale (Sammy), Freese (David, Gene, George) and Andy all-time High.

The outfield seemed very straightforward, with three candidates who stood out.

With a lot of pitchers in the pool for this team, it seemed to make sense to start with the position players and see what names were left.

The short list of players by position was as follows:

Position	Last	First	Given	Term
1B	Bright	Harry	Harry James	Bright
1B	Hale	Bob	Robert Houston	Hail
1B	Snow	J. T.	Jack Thomas	Snow
2B	Hale	Odell	Arvel Odell	Hail
2B	Hale	Chip	Walter William	Hail
2B	Lowe	Bobby	Robert Lincoln	Low
3B	Freese	David	David Richard	Freeze
3B	Freese	Gene	Eugene Lewis	Freeze
3B	Freese	George	George Walter	Freeze
3B	Hale	Sammy	Samuel Douglas	Hail
3B	High	Andy	Andrew Aird	High
C	Easterly	Ted	Theodore Harrison	Easterly
CF	Flood	Curt	Curtis Charles	Flood
LF	Cooley	Duff	Duff Gordon	Cool
LF	Raines	Tim	Timothy	Rain
OF	Weatherly	Roy	Cyril Roy	Weather
RF	Clemente	Roberto	Roberto	Clement
RF	Summers	Champ	John Junior	Summer
P	Clear	Mark	Mark Alan	Clear
P	Clement	Matt	Matthew Paul	Clement
P	Clements	Pat	Patrick Brian	Clement
P	Day	Pea Ridge	Henry Clyde	Day

Position	Last	First	Given	Term
P	Dayley	Ken	Kenneth Grant	Day
P	Drysdale	Don	Donald Scott	Dry
P	Fogg	Josh	Joshua Smith	Fogg
P	Gale	Rich	Richard Blackwell	Gale
P	Galehouse	Denny	Dennis Ward	Gale
P	Heaton	Neal	Neal	Heat
P	Hoyt	LaMarr	Dewey LaMarr	Dew
P	Lowe	Derek	Derek Christopher	Low
P	Lowe	Mark	Mark Christopher	Low
P	Spring	Jack	Jack Russell	Spring
P	Springer	Dennis	Dennis LeRoy	Spring
P	Springer	Russ	Russell Paul	Spring
P	Warmoth	Cy	Wallace Walter	Warm
P	Winter	George	George Lovington	Winter
RP	Dewey	Mark	Mark Alan	Dew
RP	Easterly	Jamie	James Morris	Easterly
RP	Weathers	David	John David	Weather

The Final Team

The Pitching Staff

Starting Pitcher 1 – Don Drysdale. No rain means it's dry, and this pitcher Dries out the bats, as evidenced by his Hall of Fame career of 209-166 and 2.95 ERA.

Starting Pitcher 2 – George Winter. Winter is here. Despite a losing record of 83 – 102, Winter's career ERA of 2.87 over 1,600 innings earned him my selection.

Starting Pitcher 3 – Dewey Hoyt. Dewey went by his middle name of LaMarr, but thankfully for this team, his real name is Dewey. His 98-68 career mark and 3.99 ERA earned him a spot on the All-Time Weather Team.

Starting Pitcher 4 – David Weathers. It seems only appropriate to have a Weathers on the Weather Team. While primarily a relief pitcher, Weathers still managed to win 73 games against 88 losses, to go along with a 4.25 ERA in 1,376 innings.

Starting Pitcher 5 –Denny Galehouse. Gale-force winds can destroy a house, but this team's glad to have a Galehouse. This weather-related pitcher won over 100 games (109-118), while compiling a 3.97 ERA over 2,004 innings.

Closer – Mark Clear. It is clear skies for this relief pitcher. He is second among weather-named players in saves, with 83, but he got the nod over Derek Lowe, since I needed another Lowe elsewhere (as discussed below). Clear finished his career with a 71 – 49 record and a 3.85 ERA. He struck out 804 batters in 804 innings.

The Outfield

Center Field – Curt Flood. Some will say that Flood caused damage by ushering in free agency and changing the dynamics of the game. Nonetheless, with 1,861 hits, a .293 batting average and a .342 on-base percentage, he is a worthy addition to the All-Time Weather Team.

Right Field – Roberto Clemente. Clement stands for mild weather, but Clemente was not mild to the competition. He is a Hall of Famer who finished his career with 3,000 hits, 240 home runs, a .317 batting average and a .359 on-base percentage.

Left Field – Tim Raines. When it pours, it rains, and there is no better rain man than Tim Raines. Besides, if you have a Flood, you must have Raines. Raines finished his career with 2,605 hits, a .294 batting average, a .380 on-base percentage and 808 stolen bases (which ranks fifth all-time). [NOTE: Consider repositioning, now that Raines has made the HOF.]

The Infield

Catcher – Ted Easterly. This wind was the easiest choice, as he was the only weather-named catcher. As a part-time catcher, Easterly finished his brief career with a .296 batting average and a .326 on-base percentage.

First Base – J.T. Snow. We have Raines, so we might as well have Snow. Snow finished his career with 1,509 hits, 189 home runs, a .268 batting average and a .357 on-base percentage. He also was a six-time Gold Glove winner.

Second Base – Odell Hale. Time for more precipitation, folks – in this case, hail in the form of Odell Hale. This Hale eliminated other Hales from consideration. Odell finished his career with 1,071 hits, a .289 batting average (among the top 500 of all-time) and a .352 on-base percentage.

Shortstop – Bobby Lowe. With no other viable options at shortstop, I selected Bobby Lowe. While primarily a second baseman, Bobby did spend some time at short and for that reason, he made the team at the expense of Derek Lowe at pitcher. Bobby was no slouch, as he finished his career with 1,929 hits, 302 stolen bases, a .273 batting average and a .325 on-base percentage.

Third Base – Andy High. Now that it had a Lowe, this team needed a High as well – so enter Andy High. His .284 career batting average places him among the top 500 of all-time. He also amassed 1,250 hits and finished with a .350 career on-base percentage.

Chapter Fifteen
The All-Time Z Team

Overview

This team consists solely of players whose last names begin with the letter "Z."

Fun Facts
- As of [2015], [88] individuals whose last names began with the letter "Z" have been credited with playing in the Major Leagues (including pre-1900).
- These [88] Z players' names reflect [70] unique names/spellings.
- No Hall of Famer has a last name beginning with the letter "Z."
- Alphabetically, Adrian Zabala appears first on the list of Z players, while Tony Zynch appears last on the list.
- Zimmerman is the most popular Z player name, with eight (nine if you count the "Zimmermann" spelling as well).
- Brad Ziegler and Zip Zabel are the only Z players to appear among the top-500 career ERA leaders.
- No Z players appear among the top-500 career batting leaders.
- Todd Ziele leads all Z players in career home runs, with 253.
- Only four Z-named pitchers have had at least 100 career wins: Tom Zachary (186), Barry Zito (165), Carlos Zambrano (132) and Geoff Zahn (111). While Tom

Zachary leads all Z pitchers with 186 career wins, he also leads all Z pitchers with 191 career losses.

Thought Process on Team Selection

With a pool of only 88 players and 70 unique names, this process seemed like a fairly straightforward effort. My approach was first to sort all of the players by their primary positions and confirm that all positions were covered. This step showed that of the 88 players, 45 were position players and 43 were pitchers. Examining the career stats surfaced many position players with fewer than 100 career hits and many pitchers with fewer than 100 career innings pitched. I eliminated those players with short careers to see if a viable pool of players remained. I was left with 22 pitchers and 19 position players – and, most importantly, all positions were represented.

With multiple Zimmermans on the list, I knew I had to pay special attention to finding the best one and still fill out all positions. I also noticed that Ben Zobrist seemed like a potential fit for the team. Since he plays multiple positions, determining which position he should fill was also an important consideration.

Finding the best five out of 22 pitchers still in the mix seemed like a fairly straightforward exercise.

Overall, the list of players with at least 100 career hits or 100 career innings pitch includes:

Last	First	Pos.	AB	H	HR	BA	OBA
Zarilla	**Al**	**OF**	**3535**	**975**	**61**	**0.276**	**0.357**
Zauchin	Norm	1B	1038	242	50	0.233	0.324
Zaun	Gregg	C	3489	878	88	0.252	0.344
Zeider	Rollie	2B	2264	533	4	0.235	0.314
Zeile	**Todd**	**3B**	**7573**	**2004**	**253**	**0.265**	**0.346**
Zernial	**Gus**	**LF**	**4131**	**1093**	**237**	**0.265**	**0.329**
Zientara	Benny	2B	906	230	2	0.254	0.293
Zimmer	Don	3B	3283	773	91	0.235	0.29
Zimmer	**Chief**	**C**	**4263**	**1159**	**26**	**0.272**	**0.342**
Zimmerman	Jerry	C	994	203	3	0.204	0.269
Zimmerman	**Ryan**	**1B, 3B**	**5416**	**1505**	**215**	**0.278**	**0.343**
Zimmerman	Heinie	3B	5304	1566	58	0.295	0.331
Zinn	Guy	OF	566	150	7	0.265	0.337
Zisk	**Richie**	**RF**	**5144**	**1477**	**207**	**0.287**	**0.353**
Zitzmann	**Billy**	**OF**	**1004**	**268**	**3**	**0.267**	**0.333**
Zobrist	**Ben**	**2B, SS, OF**	**4840**	**1287**	**145**	**0.266**	**0.358**
Zunino	Mike	C	1125	219	50	0.195	0.262
Zupcic	Bob	OF	795	199	7	0.250	0.303
Zuvella	Paul	SS	491	109	2	0.222	0.275

Last	First	IP	W	L	ERA	Saves
Zabel	Zip	296	12	14	2.71	3
Zachary	Chris	321.1	10	29	4.57	2
Zachary	Tom	3126.1	186	191	3.73	22
Zachry	Pat	1177.1	69	67	3.52	3
Zahn	Geoff	1849	111	109	3.74	1
Zahniser	Paul	618.2	25	47	4.66	1

Last	First	IP	W	L	ERA	Saves
Zambrano	Victor	706.1	45	44	4.64	3
Zambrano	Carlos	1959	132	91	3.66	0
Zamora	Oscar	224.2	13	14	4.53	23
Zanni	Dom	183	9	6	3.79	10
Zepp	Bill	188	10	5	3.64	4
Zerbe	Chad	151	6	1	3.87	0
Zettlein	George	234	4	20	3.88	2
Ziegler	Brad	596.2	34	28	2.44	85
Zimmerman	Jeff	228.2	17	12	3.27	32
Zimmermann	Jordan	1199.1	79	57	3.45	0
Zinn	Jimmy	299	13	16	4.3	7
Zito	Barry	2576.2	165	143	4.04	0
Zoldak	Sam	929.1	43	53	3.54	8
Zuber	Bill	786	43	42	4.28	6
Zumaya	Joel	209.2	13	12	3.05	5
Zuverink	George	642.1	32	36	3.54	40

The Final Team

The Pitching Staff

Starting Pitcher 1 – Carlos Zambrano. Carlos posted only the third-leading win total among all Z pitchers but had the best ERA and winning percentage among the Z-named pitchers with 100 or more wins. Overall, he was 132-91 with a 3.66 ERA.

Starting Pitcher 2 – Barry Zito. Barry ranks second all-time in career wins among Z-named pitchers. His career record was 165-143. In 2002, he won the American League Cy Young Award, with a 23-5 record and a 2.75 ERA.

Starting Pitcher 3 – Geoff Zahn. Geoff finished his career with a 111-109 record and a respectable 3.74 ERA.

Starting Pitcher 4 – Tom Zachary. The career win (and loss) leader among Z-named players, Tom is slotted as the number 4 starter on the All-Time Z Team. While his career ERA of 3.73 is higher than that of a similarly-named player Pat Zachry (3.52), I selected Tom Zachary based on his longevity (3,126 career innings versus 1,177 for Pat Zachry).

Starting Pitcher 5 – Zip Zabel. The fifth starter was the most difficult to select. Three pitchers – Victor Zambrano, Pat Zachry and Jordan Zimmerman – would easily be selected over Zabel, if not for the fact that their names had to be used to fill other positions. Zabel had only 25 career starts and 296 innings pitched, but my decision to select Zabel came down to the fact that his 2.71 ERA ranks him among the top [500] all-time ERA leaders (albeit based on a small sample).

Closer – Brad Ziegler. Brad is still active and, with [85] saves, is already the career saves leader among Z-named pitchers. He, too, currently sits among the top 500 career ERA leaders, with a lifetime ERA of 2.44.

The Outfield

Center Field – Al Zarilla. Zarilla played all three outfield positions during his 10-year career. He finished with a career .276 batting average and solid .357 on-base percentage.

Right Field – Richie Zisk. Zisk is the leading hitter among Z-named players, with a career .287 batting average. He also had 207 career homers and a .353 career on-base percentage.

Left Field – Gus Zernial. Zernial ranks second all-time in home runs by Z-named players, with 237. He finished his career with a .265 batting average and a .329 on-base percentage.

The Infield

Catcher – Chief Zimmer. Catcher was a tough choice. I selected Zimmer over Gregg Zaun, despite their similar statistics. Zaun finished with a career .252 batting average and .344 on-base percentage. Zimmer had 1,159 career hits (as compared to 878 for Zaun), a .272 batting average and a .342 on-base percentage. While Zaun had more home runs (88 to 26), I placed more emphasis on batting average than power numbers (which, while greater for Zaun, were not significant for either player).

First Base – Ryan Zimmerman. An active player with [over 1,500] career hits to date. Ryan came up as a third baseman and was the Nationals' first draft pick after the team moved to Washington from Montreal. He currently has a [.278] career batting average, along with a [.343] on-base percentage. I decided to keep him at his current position.

Second Base – Rollie Zeider. Second base basically came down to three players, pending a related decision on where to play Ben Zobrist. The other candidates included Benny Zientara and Paul Zuvella. Zientara was a second baseman with a respectable .254 batting average but only 906 career at-bats. Zuvella was a shortstop with only 109 career hits. Once I decided that both Zientara and Zeider were better choices than Zuvella, it helped seal the selection of Zobrist at shortstop and, in the end, I felt Zeider's greater longevity outweighed Zientara's better batting average.

Shortstop – Ben Zobrist. Zobrist is another active player whose career hits and home run totals will only increase. He currently has [1,287] career hits and [145] career home runs, along with a [.266] batting average and a [.358] on-base percentage that currently leads all Z-named players.

Third Base – Todd Zeile. Zeile is the career Z-named home run leader (253) and hit leader (2,004). He finished his career with a .265 batting average and a .346 on-base percentage.

Chapter Sixteen
The All-Time Automotive Team

Overview

This team includes players with surnames which, when pronounced, contain a type of car, truck or motorcycle brand, manufacturer or generic name (*e.g.*, Mercedes, Benz, Ford, Harley, van, car, bus), an automotive part, including manufacturers of parts (*e.g.*, wheel, cam, tire, Dunlop, Goodyear, key), or an automotive term (*e.g.*, rig, stall, heap).

The spelling does not need to be an exact match (*e.g.*, Axel instead of Axle) but the pronunciation does.

I erred on the side of fewer players if I had any doubts about correct pronunciations of names. For example, Adrian Beltre and Carlos Beltran were not considered to represent "belt," as the pronunciation in each case is more like "Bell-Tray" and "Bell – Tran."

In the event of multiple player name matches to the same automotive-related term, I gave preference to players whose complete surnames exactly matched the given term in pronunciation. For example, a player with the name Dodge took priority over a player with the name Dodgey, such that only the player(s) with the name Dodge would be considered in that instance.

I used the following list of 90 automotive terms to qualify players for this team:

Acura	Chrysler	Filter	**Key**	Peugeot	**Stall**
Austin	**Cog**	Ford	Kia	**Pickup**	**Steer**
Axle	**Coil**	Garage	Lamborghini	**Pillion**	**Suzuki**
Belt	Daewoo	**Gas**	Lexus	**Pinto**	Tahoe
Bentley	**Dash**	Gear	**Lincoln**	Pirelli	**Tank**
Benz	**Dent**	Goodyear	**Lube**	Piston	Tire
Brake	**Diesel**	Hankook	**Mack**	Porsche	Toyota
Buick	**Dodge**	Harley	Maserati	**Rig**	Traverse
Bus	**Dunlop**	**Heap**	**Mercedes**	**Ryder**	**Tread**
Cab	**Durango**	**Hudson**	Miata	Saab	**Truck**
Cam	Edsel	Hyundai	Michelen	**Sasaki**	Valve
Camaro	Engine	Impala	Motor	**Sebring**	**Van**
Car	Exhaust	Jaguar	Nissan	Semi	Volvo
Carerra	**Ferrari**	Jeep	**Oil**	**Skid**	**Wheel**
Chevrolet	Fiat	**Kawasaki**	**Packard**	**Speed**	Yamaha

Fun Facts

- The surnames of over 300 Major League Baseball players encompass 51 of the 90 automotive terms.
- Ford is the second-most common automotive term contained within player surnames, represented by 78 players. The most popular names among those 78 players are 17 Fords, 17 Crawfords, five Sanfords and five Staffords.
- Van is the next most-common automotive term among player surnames (45 players).

- Fittingly, Car is also a popular automotive name (37 players).
- The automotive list features two Hall of Famers – pitcher Whitey Ford and manager Connie Mack. Two members whose surnames have automotive connotations but are not on the qualifying list for this team are Bob Lemon and Andy "Mini" Cooper.

Thought Process on Team Selection

The entire pool of automotive players (including those from prior to 1900), based on the eligible automotive terms listed above, was the following:

Last Name	First Name	Given Name	Term
Austin	Henry	Henry C.	AUSTIN
Austin	Jim	James Parker	AUSTIN
Austin	Jimmy	James Philip	AUSTIN
Austin	Jeff	Jeffrey Wellington	AUSTIN
Austin	Rick	Rick Gerald	AUSTIN
Axelrod	Dylan	Dylan Davis Haines	AXLE
Belt	Brandon	Brandon Kyle	BELT
Bentley	Cy	Clytus George	BENTLEY
Bentley	Jack	John Needles	BENTLEY
Benz	Joe	Joseph Louis	BENZ
Benzinger	Todd	Todd Eric	BENZ
DeBus	Adam	Adam Joseph	BUS
Jacobus	Larry	Stuart Louis	BUS
Phoebus	Tom	Thomas Harold	BUS
Buskey	Joe	Joseph Henry	BUS, KEY
Buskey	Mike	Michael Thomas	BUS, KEY
Buskey	Tom	Thomas William	BUS, KEY

Last Name	First Name	Given Name	Term
Buss	Nick	Nicholas Gregory	BUS
Kucab	Johnny	John Albert	CAB
Cambria	Fred	Frederick Dennis	CAM
Camelli	Hank	Henry Richard	CAM
Cameron	Jack	John Stanley	CAM
Cameron	Kevin	Kevin John	CAM
Cameron	Mike	Michael Terrance	CAM
Camilli	Dolph	Adolph Louis	CAM
Camilli	Doug	Douglas Joseph	CAM
Camilli	Lou	Louis Steven	CAM
Caminero	Arquimedes	Arquimedes Euclides	CAM
Caminiti	Ken	Kenneth Gene	CAM
Cammack	Eric	Eric Wade	CAM
Camnitz	Harry	Henry Richardson	CAM
Camnitz	Howie	Samuel Howard	CAM
Kamieniecki	Scott	Scott Andrew	CAM
Kamm	Willie	William Edward	CAM
Kammeyer	Bob	Robert Lynn	CAM
Accardo	Jeremy	Jeremiah Lee	CAR
Azocar	Oscar	Oscar Gregorio	CAR
Carbine	John	John C.	CAR
Carbo	Bernie	Bernardo	CAR
Carden	John	John Bruton	CAR
Cardenal	Jose	Jose Rosario Domec	CAR
Cardenas	Adrian	Adrian	CAR
Cardenas	Leo	Leonardo Lazaro	CAR
Cardinal	Conrad	Conrad Seth	CAR
Cardona	Javier	Javier Peterson	CAR
Cardoni	Ben	Armand Joseph	CAR

Last Name	First Name	Given Name	Term
Carfrey	Ed	Edwin M.	CAR
Cargo	Bobby	Robert J.	CAR
Carman	Don	Donald Wayne	CAR
Carman	George	George Wartman	CAR
Carpenter	Drew	Andrew James Rudolph	CAR
Carpenter	Bubba	Charles Sydney	CAR
Carpenter	Chris	Christopher John	CAR
Carpenter	Chris	Christopher John	CAR
Carpenter	Cris	Cris Howell	CAR
Carpenter	David	Darrell David	CAR
Carpenter	David	David Lee	CAR
Carpenter	Lew	Lewis Emmett	CAR
Carpenter	Matt	Matthew Martin	CAR
Carpenter	Paul	Paul Calvin	CAR
Carpenter	Bob	Robert Louis	CAR
Carpenter	Hick	Warren William	CAR
Carpin	Frank	Frank Dominic	CAR
Carr	Charlie	Charles Carbitt	CAR
Carr	Chuck	Charles Lee Glenn	CAR
Carr	Lew	Lewis Smith	CAR
Delcarmen	Manny	Manuel	CAR
Kardow	Paul	Paul Otto	CAR
Karlon	Bill	William John	CAR
Karr	Benn	Benjamin Joyce	CAR
Karsay	Steve	Stefan Andrew	CAR
Karstens	Jeff	Jeffrey Wayne	CAR
Carrara	Giovanni	Giovanni	CARRERA
Carrera	Ezequiel	Ezequiel Manuel	CARRERA
Cogan	Tony	Anthony Michael	COG
Cogan	Dick	Richard Henry	COG

Last Name	First Name	Given Name	Term
Coggin	Dave	David Raymond	COG
Coggins	Frank	Franklin	COG
Coggins	Rich	Richard Allen	COG
Cogswell	Ed	Edward	COG
Coyle	Bill	William Claude	COIL
Dashiell	Wally	John Wallace	DASH
Dashner	Lee	Lee Claire	DASH
Dent	Eddie	Elliott Estill	DENT
Dent	Bucky	Russell Earl	DENT
Dente	Sam	Samuel Joseph	DENT
Deisel	Pat	Edward	DIESEL
Dodge	John	John Lewis	DODGE
Dodge	Sam	Samuel Edward	DODGE
Dunlop	George	George Henry	DUNLOP
Durango	Luis	Luis A.	DURANGO
Ferrari	Anthony	Anthony Michael	FERRARI
Ashford	Tucker	Thomas Steven	FORD
Axford	John	John Berton	FORD
Bedford	Gene	William Eugene	FORD
Bickford	Vern	Vernon Edgell	FORD
Bradford	Chad	Chadwick Lee	FORD
Bradford	Buddy	Charles William	FORD
Bradford	Vic	Henry Victor	FORD
Bradford	Larry	Larry	FORD
Bradford	Bill	William D.	FORD
Crawford	Brandon	Brandon Michael	FORD
Crawford	Carl	Carl Demonte	FORD
Crawford	Carlos	Carlos Lamonte	FORD
Crawford	Larry	Charles Lowrie	FORD
Crawford	Pat	Clifford Rankin	FORD
Crawford	Evan	Evan Shane	FORD

Last Name	First Name	Given Name	Term
Crawford	Forrest	Forrest A.	FORD
Crawford	George	George	FORD
Crawford	Glenn	Glenn Martin	FORD
Crawford	Jim	James Frederick	FORD
Crawford	Joe	Joseph Randal	FORD
Crawford	Ken	Kenneth Daniel	FORD
Crawford	Paxton	Paxton Keith	FORD
Crawford	Jake	Rufus	FORD
Crawford	Sam	Samuel Earl	FORD
Crawford	Steve	Steven Ray	FORD
Crawford	Willie	Willie Murphy	FORD
Ford	Ben	Benjamin Cooper	FORD
Ford	Curt	Curtis Glenn	FORD
Ford	Dan	Darnell Glenn	FORD
Ford	Darren	Darren Scott	FORD
Ford	Dave	David Alan	FORD
Ford	Ed	Edgar Lee	FORD
Ford	Whitey	Edward Charles	FORD
Ford	Gene	Eugene Matthew	FORD
Ford	Gene	Eugene Wyman	FORD
Ford	Hod	Horace Hills	FORD
Ford	Lew	Jon Lewis	FORD
Ford	Matt	Matthew Lee	FORD
Ford	Wenty	Percival Edmund Wentworth	FORD
Ford	Russ	Russell William	FORD
Ford	Ted	Theodore Henry	FORD
Ford	Tom	Thomas Walter	FORD
Ford	William	William Brown	FORD
Fordham	Tom	Thomas James	FORD
Hafford	Leo	Leo Edgar	FORD

Last Name	First Name	Given Name	Term
Hartford	Bruce	Bruce Daniel	FORD
Langford	Sam	Elton	FORD
Langford	Rick	James Rick	FORD
Langsford	Bob	Robert William	FORD
Lankford	Frank	Frank Greenfield	FORD
Lankford	Ray	Raymond Lewis	FORD
Lansford	Carney	Carney Ray	FORD
Lansford	Joe	Joseph Dale	FORD
Lunsford	Trey	James Lewis	FORD
Moford	Herb	Herbert	FORD
Pickford	Kevin	Kevin Patrick	FORD
Radford	Paul	Paul Revere	FORD
Relaford	Desi	Desmond Lamont	FORD
Rushford	Jim	James Thomas	FORD
Rutherford	Jim	James Hollis	FORD
Rutherford	Johnny	John William	FORD
Sanford	Chance	Chance Steven	FORD
Sanford	Jack	John Doward	FORD
Sanford	Fred	John Frederick	FORD
Sanford	Jack	John Stanley	FORD
Sanford	Mo	Meredith Leroy	FORD
Shackelford	Brian	Brian Wesley	FORD
Stafford	Heinie	Henry Alexander	FORD
Stafford	General	James Joseph	FORD
Stafford	John	John Henry	FORD
Stafford	Bill	William Charles	FORD
Stafford			FORD
Stanford	Jason	Jason John	FORD
Teaford	Everett	Everett James	FORD
Telford	Anthony	Anthony Charles	FORD
Winford	Jim	James Head	FORD

Last Name	First Name	Given Name	Term
Wohlford	Jim	James Eugene	FORD
Garagiola	Joe	Joseph Henry	GARAGE
Fabregas	Jorge	Jorge	GAS
Gaspar	Harry	Harry Lambert	GAS
Gaspar	Rod	Rodney Earl	GAS
Gassaway	Charlie	Charles Cason	GAS
Gassner	Dave	David K.	GAS
Gastall	Tom	Thomas Everett	GAS
Gaston	Alex	Alexander Nathaniel	GAS
Gaston	Cito	Clarence Edwin	GAS
Gaston	Milt	Nathaniel Milton	GAS
Gaston	Welcome	Welcome Thornburg	GAS
Villegas	Ismael	Ismael	GAS
Gear	Dale	Dale Dudley	GEAR
Gearhart	Gary	Lloyd William	GEAR
Gearin	Dinty	Dennis John	GEAR
Gearrin	Cory	Cory Nathanial	GEAR
Geary	Huck	Eugene Francis Joseph	GEAR
Geary	Geoff	Geoffrey Michael	GEAR
Geary	Bob	Robert Norton	GEAR
Geer	Josh	Joshua Brent	GEAR
Geer	Billy	William Henry Harrison	GEAR
Harley	Dick	Henry Risk	HARLEY
Harley	Dick	Richard Joseph	HARLEY
Heep	Danny	Daniel William	HEEP
Hudson	Charlie	Charles	HUDSON
Hudson	Charles	Charles Lynn	HUDSON
Hudson	Daniel	Daniel Claiborne	HUDSON

Last Name	First Name	Given Name	Term
Hudson	Hal	Hal Campbell	HUDSON
Hudson	Jesse	Jesse James	HUDSON
Hudson	Johnny	John Wilson	HUDSON
Hudson	Joe	Joseph Paul	HUDSON
Hudson	Kyle	Kyle Jordan	HUDSON
Hudson	Luke	Luke Stephen	HUDSON
Hudson	Nat	Nathaniel P.	HUDSON
Hudson	Orlando	Orlando Thill	HUDSON
Hudson	Rex	Rex Haughton	HUDSON
Hudson	Sid	Sidney Charles	HUDSON
Kawasaki	Munenori	Munenori	KAWASAKI
Bronkey	Jeff	Jacob Jeffery	KEY
Caskey	Craig	Craig Douglas	KEY
Key	Jimmy	James Edward	KEY
Lincoln	Brad	Brad Eric	LINCOLN
Lincoln	Ezra	Ezra Perry	LINCOLN
Lincoln	Mike	Michael George	LINCOLN
Luebbe	Roy	Roy John	LUBE
Mack	Connie	Cornelius Alexander	MACK
Mack	Denny	Dennis Joseph	MACK
Mack	Earle	Earle Thaddeus	MACK
Mack	Frank	Frank George	MACK
Mack	Reddy	Joseph	MACK
Mack	Joe	Joseph John	MACK
Mack	Quinn	Quinn David	MACK
Mack	Ray	Raymond James	MACK
Mack	Shane	Shane Lee	MACK
Mack	Tony	Tony Lynn	MACK
Mack	Bill	William Francis	MACK
Mercedes	Henry	Henry Felipe	MERCEDES

Last Name	First Name	Given Name	Term
Mercedes	Jose	Jose Miguel	MERCEDES
Mercedes	Luis	Luis Roberto	MERCEDES
Mercedes	Melvin	Melvin	MERCEDES
Oyler	Andy	Andrew Paul	OIL
Oyler	Ray	Raymond Francis	OIL
Packard	Gene	Eugene Milo	PACKARD
Pickup	Ty	Clarence William	PICKUP
Pillion	Squiz	Cecil Randolph	PILLION
Pinto	Josmil	Josmil Oswaldo	PINTO
Pinto	Renyel	Renyel Eligio	PINTO
Pinto	Lerton	William Lerton	PINTO
Rigby	Brad	Bradley Kenneth	RIG
Rigdon	Paul	Paul David	RIG
Riggan	Jerrod	Jerrod Ashley	RIG
Riggans	Shawn	Shawn Willis	RIG
Riggert	Joe	Joseph Aloysius	RIG
Riggleman	Jim	James David	RIG
Riggs	Adam	Adam David	RIG
Riggs	Lew	Lewis Sidney	RIG
Rigney	Topper	Emory Elmo	RIG
Rigney	Johnny	John Dungan	RIG
Rigney	Bill	William Joseph	RIG
Ryder	Tom	Thomas	RYDER
Sasaki	Kazuhiro	Kazuhiro	SASAKI
Sebring	Jimmy	James Dennison	SEBRING
Skidmore	Roe	Robert Roe	SKID
Speed	Horace	Horace Arthur	SPEED
Stahl	Chick	Charles Sylvester	STALL
Stahl	Jake	Garland	STALL
Stahl	Larry	Larry Floyd	STALL
Stallard	Tracy	Evan Tracy	STALL

Last Name	First Name	Given Name	Term
Stallcup	Virgil	Thomas Virgil	STALL
Staller	George	George Walborn	STALL
Stallings	George	George Tweedy	STALL
Steere	Gene	Frederick Eugene	STEER
Suzuki	Ichiro	Ichiro	SUZUKI
Suzuki	Kurt	Kurt Kiyoshi	SUZUKI
Suzuki	Mac	Makoto	SUZUKI
Tankersley	Dennis	Dennis Lee	TANK
Tankersley	Leo	Lawrence William	TANK
Tankersley	Taylor	Taylor Mark	TANK
Treadaway	Ray	Edgar Raymond	TREAD
Treadway	George	George B.	TREAD
Treadway	Jeff	Hugh Jeffery	TREAD
Treadway	Red	Thadford Leon	TREAD
Trucks	Virgil	Virgil Oliver	TRUCKS
Bevan	Hal	Harold Joseph	VAN
Canavan	Hugh	Hugh Edward	VAN
Canavan	Jim	James Edward	VAN
DaVanon	Jerry	Frank Gerald	VAN
DaVanon	Jeff	Jeffrey Graham	VAN
Donovan	Fred	Frederick Maurice	VAN
Donovan	Jerry	Jeremiah Francis	VAN
Donovan	Mike	Michael Berchman	VAN
Donovan	Patsy	Patrick Joseph	VAN
Donovan	Dick	Richard Edward	VAN
Donovan	Tom	Thomas Joseph	VAN
Donovan	Bill	Willard Earl	VAN
Donovan	Bill	William Edward	VAN
Gallivan	Phil	Philip Joseph	VAN
Hannivan	Pat	Patrick James	VAN
Levan	Jesse	Jesse Roy	VAN

Last Name	First Name	Given Name	Term
Van Alstyne	Clay	Clayton Emory	VAN
Van Atta	Russ	Russell	VAN
Van Benschoten	John	John Wesley	VAN
Van Brabant	Ozzie	Camille Oscar	VAN
Van Buren	Deacon	Edward Eugene	VAN
Van Buren	Jermaine	Jermaine Russell	VAN
Van Burkleo	Ty	Tyler Lee	VAN
Van Camp	Al	Albert Joseph	VAN
Van Cuyk	Chris	Christian Gerald	VAN
Van Cuyk	Johnny	John Henry	VAN
van den Hurk	Rick	Henricus Nicolas	VAN
Van Dusen	Fred	Frederick William	VAN
Van Dyke	Ben	Benjamin Harrison	VAN
Van Dyke	Bill	William Jennings	VAN
Van Egmond	Tim	Timothy Layne	VAN
Van Every	Jonathan	Jonathan Eugene	VAN
Van Gorder	Dave	David Thomas	VAN
Van Haltren	George	George Edward Martin	VAN
Van Hekken	Andy	Andrew William	VAN
Van Noy	Jay	Jay Lowell	VAN
Van Poppel	Todd	Todd Matthew	VAN
Van Robays	Maurice	Maurice Rene	VAN
Van Slyke	Andy	Andrew James	VAN
Van Slyke	Scott	Scott T.	VAN
Van Zandt	Ike	Charles Isaac	VAN
Van Zant	Dick	Richard	VAN
Vangilder	Elam	Elam Russell	VAN
VanLandingham	William	William Joseph	VAN
Vann	John	John Silas	VAN

Last Name	First Name	Given Name	Term
VanRyn	Ben	Benjamin Ashley	VAN
Wheeler	Dan	Daniel Michael	WHEEL
Wheeler	Don	Donald Wesley	WHEEL
Wheeler	Ed	Edward Leroy	WHEEL
Wheeler	Ed	Edward Raymond	WHEEL
Wheeler	Rip	Floyd Clark	WHEEL
Wheeler	George	George Harrison	WHEEL
Wheeler	George	George Louis	WHEEL
Wheeler	Harry	Harry Eugene	WHEEL
Wheeler	Dick	Richard	WHEEL
Wheeler	Ryan	Ryan Gerard	WHEEL
Wheeler	Zach	Zachary Harrison	WHEEL
Wheeler	Zelous	Zelous Lamar	WHEEL
Wheelock	Gary	Gary Richard	WHEEL
Wheelock	Bobby	Warren Henry	WHEEL

My first step to reduce the overall pool was to eliminate duplicate names. I started with Ford, since Whitey Ford is a Hall of Famer whose selection, by eliminating all the other Fords, would reduce the pool size by 77.

Although an active player not yet eligible for Hall of Fame consideration, Ichiro Suzuki (motorcycle brand) is sure to be inducted eventually. Consequently, his inclusion on this team seemed obvious and eliminated other right fielders from consideration.

Selecting a short-list of "van" and "car" names also helped to reduce the pool size. Since several of the derived "car" names (like Carpenter) seemed like a stretch anyway, I decided to limit my consideration of "car" names to those players whose entire surname seemed more of a fit, such as Carr, Karr, Carman and Carpin).

Similarly restricting the other names to more exact matches with the list of eligible automotive terms, as well as eliminating pre-1900 players and players with limited Major League experience (unless they represented the only name for a given term) reduced the pool to under 100 players.

I then sorted the pool by position, validating that all the positions were covered.

The new list looked like this:

POS	Last Name	First Name	Given Name	Term
1B	Belt	Brandon	Brandon Kyle	BELT
1B	Benzinger	Todd	Todd Eric	BENZ
1B	Stahl	Jake	Garland	STALL
2B	Hudson	Johnny	John Wilson	HUDSON
2B	Hudson	Orlando	Orlando Thill	HUDSON
2B	Mack	Ray	Raymond James	MACK
2B	Treadway	Jeff	Hugh Jeffery	TREAD
3B	Austin	Jimmy	James Philip	AUSTIN
3B	Kamm	Willie	William Edward	CAM
3B	Dodge	John	John Lewis	DODGE
3B	Riggs	Lew	Lewis Sidney	RIG
3B	Bevan	Hal	Harold Joseph	VAN
3B	Levan	Jesse	Jesse Roy	VAN
C	Deisel	Pat	Edward	DIESEL
C	Garagiola	Joe	Joseph Henry	GARAGE
C	Fabregas	Jorge	Jorge	GAS

POS	Last Name	First Name	Given Name	Term
C	Gaston	Alex	Alexander Nathaniel	GAS
C	Luebbe	Roy	Roy John	LUBE
C	Mercedes	Henry	Henry Felipe	MERCEDES
C	Pinto	Josmil	Josmil Oswaldo	PINTO
C	Suzuki	Kurt	Kurt Kiyoshi	SUZUKI
CF	Carr	Chuck	Charles Lee Glenn	CAR
CF	Gaston	Cito	Clarence Edwin	GAS
CF	Gearhart	Gary	Lloyd William	GEAR
CF	Van Slyke	Andy	Andrew James	VAN
LF	Buss	Nick	Nicholas Gregory	BUS
LF	Durango	Luis	Luis A.	DURANGO
LF	Harley	Dick	Richard Joseph	HARLEY
LF	Mack	Shane	Shane Lee	MACK
OF	Pickup	Ty	Clarence William	PICKUP
OF	Ryder	Tom	Thomas	RYDER
OF	Sebring	Jimmy	James Dennison	SEBRING
OF	Speed	Horace	Horace Arthur	SPEED
OF	Stahl	Larry	Larry Floyd	STALL
OF	Van Robays	Maurice	Maurice Rene	VAN
P	Axelrod	Dylan	Dylan Davis Haines	AXLE
P	Bentley	Jack	John Needles	BENTLEY
P	Benz	Joe	Joseph Louis	BENZ
P	Phoebus	Tom	Thomas Harold	BUS
P	Kucab	Johnny	John Albert	CAB
P	Carman	Don	Donald Wayne	CAR
P	Karr	Benn	Benjamin Joyce	CAR
P	Dodge	Sam	Samuel Edward	DODGE
P	Ferrari	Anthony	Anthony Michael	FERRARI
P	Ford	Whitey	Edward Charles	FORD
P	Gaspar	Harry	Harry Lambert	GAS

POS	Last Name	First Name	Given Name	Term
P	Gaston	Milt	Nathaniel Milton	GAS
P	Gear	Dale	Dale Dudley	GEAR
P	Gearin	Dinty	Dennis John	GEAR
P	Gearrin	Cory	Cory Nathanial	GEAR
P	Geary	Geoff	Geoffrey Michael	GEAR
P	Hudson	Charles	Charles Lynn	HUDSON
P	Hudson	Joe	Joseph Paul	HUDSON
P	Hudson	Sid	Sidney Charles	HUDSON
P	Key	Jimmy	James Edward	KEY
P	Lincoln	Brad	Brad Eric	LINCOLN
P	Lincoln	Mike	Michael George	LINCOLN
P	Mercedes	Jose	Jose Miguel	MERCEDES
P	Packard	Gene	Eugene Milo	PACKARD
P	Pillion	Squiz	Cecil Randolph	PILLION
P	Pinto	Renyel	Renyel Eligio	PINTO
P	Pinto	Lerton	William Lerton	PINTO
P	Sasaki	Kazuhiro	Kazuhiro	SASAKI
P	Stallard	Tracy	Evan Tracy	STALL
P	Tankersley	Dennis	Dennis Lee	TANK
P	Tankersley	Taylor	Taylor Mark	TANK
P	Trucks	Virgil	Virgil Oliver	TRUCKS
P	Van Poppel	Todd	Todd Matthew	VAN
P	Wheelock	Gary	Gary Richard	WHEEL
P, RP	Hudson	Daniel	Daniel Claiborne	HUDSON
PH	Skidmore	Roe	Robert Roe	SKID
PH	Vann	John	John Silas	VAN
RF	Suzuki	Ichiro	Ichiro	SUZUKI
RP	Buskey	Tom	Thomas William	BUS, KEY
RP	Delcarmen	Manny	Manuel	CAR
RP	Carrara	Giovanni	Giovanni	CARRERA

POS	Last Name	First Name	Given Name	Term
RP	Wheeler	Dan	Daniel Michael	WHEEL
SS	Dashiell	Wally	John Wallace	DASH
SS	Dent	Bucky	Russell Earl	DENT
SS	Dente	Sam	Samuel Joseph	DENT
SS	Dunlop	George	George Henry	DUNLOP
SS	Geary	Huck	Eugene Francis Joseph	GEAR
SS	Kawasaki	Munenori	Munenori	KAWASAKI
SS	Oyler	Ray	Raymond Francis	OIL
SS	Stallcup	Virgil	Thomas Virgil	STALL
SS	Steere	Gene	Frederick Eugene	STEER

At first base, the choice came down to Brandon "Fan" Belt, Todd Benz(inger) and Jake Stahl. Given the other "Benz" and "stall" players, inclusion of Benzinger and/or Stahl would eliminate other candidates from contention for this team.

Selection for second base seemed like a contest between a tread (Jeff Treadway) and a couple of Hudsons (Orlando and Johnny).

At third base, the short list included a cam (Willie Kamm) and an Austin (Jimmy Austin).

At shortstop, I spotted a couple of Dents.

The pool of pitching candidates offered the most optionality, so it made sense to start by analyzing this team's position player prospects.

Among the pitchers, beyond the standout Whitey Ford, a few of them seemed like they were going to be logical choices, based on longevity.

The Final Team

The Pitching Staff

Starting Pitcher 1 – Whitey Ford. The "Chairman of the Board," this Ford ranks third all-time in winning percentage (.690), with a career record of 236-106 and a 2.75 ERA.

Starting Pitcher 2 – Jimmy Key. The Key to this automotive selection is his 186-117 career record.

Starting Pitcher 3 – Virgil Trucks. The Trucks stops here as this team's number three starter. Virgil finished his career with 177 wins against 135 losses and a 3.39 ERA.

Starting Pitcher 4 – Joe Benz. This luxury vehicle got the nod as the number 4 starter with his outstanding career ERA of 2.43. Benz's ERA ranks among the top 100 of all-time (though it somehow earned him only a 77-75 lifetime won/loss record).

Starting Pitcher 5 – Tom Phoebus. I selected this bus over two classics, a Packard (Gene) and a Hudson (Tim). Phoebus finished his career with a 56-52 record and a 3.33 ERA. This was similar to Packard's 45-43 record and 3.17 ERA. I decided to save the "Hudson" name for another position and picked the Phoebus over Packard because of the former's larger strikeout totals (725 versus 226).

Closer – Dan Wheeler. You can't drive a car without a wheel, and this Wheel(er) won out over Manny Delcarmen. Wheeler finished with only 43 career saves, but that marked the most by any automotive relief pitcher.

The Outfield

Center Field – Andy Van Slyke. I rode this Van (Slyke) based on his 1,562 career hits, .274 batting average and .349 on-base percentage.

Right Field –Ichiro Suzuki. This motorcycle-named speedster is sure to be a Hall of Famer. He currently has [3,030] hits, 508 stolen bases, a [.313] batting average and a [.356] on-base percentage.

Left Field – Shane Mack. This truck finished his 11-year career with a .299 batting average and .364 on-base percentage.

The Infield

Catcher – Joe Garagiola. An automotive team is not complete without a place to park, so I took this garage-named backstop. Joe finished his career with a .257 batting average and .354 on-base percentage.

First Base – Brandon Belt. I opted for an active player at first base, based on his current [80] home runs and [.818] OPS, including his [.272] batting average and [.359] on-base percentage.

Second Base – Orlando Hudson. I selected this classic car over Jeff Treadway. Hudson finished his career with 93 home runs, a .273 batting average and a .341 on-base percentage.

Shortstop – Bucky Dent. Bucky dings up this automotive team by having amassed 1,114 career hits. His career batting average of .247 is respectable for a shortstop of his generation. Of course, he will forever be hated by Red Sox fans for his home run to win the American League Eastern division title for the Yankees in 1978.

Third Base – Willie Kamm. Cams enhance an engine's performance, and this Kamm certainly helps the automotive team. Willie finished his career with 1,643 hits, a .281 batting average and a .372 on-base percentage.

Chapter Seventeen
The All-Time All Berry Team

Overview

To qualify for this team, a player must have "berry," "bery" or "berie" in his last name. I eliminated players with names containing components sounding like "berry," such as "bury."

Fun Facts

- Only 30 players in Major League history have had some form of "berry" in their names, 11 of whom have had the last name of "Berry."
- The pool of "berry" players includes two father/son pairs – John Mayberry Sr. and Jr. and Joseph Berry Sr. and Jr.
- The Joseph Berry duo combined for a lifetime batting average of .300 and on-base percentage of .416. Unfortunately, their combined at-bats totaled only 10, with three hits between the two of them.
- Darryl Strawberry is the all-time leader in berry-named player home runs, with 335, and hits, with 1,401.
- Sean Berry edges out Bret Barberie as the all-time berry-named batting leader (.272 to .271) among players with a minimum of 1,000 career at-bats.

Thought Process on Team Selection

With such a small pool of berry-named players, the paramount challenge in forming this all-time team was not to repeat a name. With 11 players named Berry, selecting just one of them meant that the remaining pool of players would drop to 19. After accounting for the other duplicate berry names, that number dropped further to only 17 unique names for 14 positions.

The obvious choices from the list of available players were Darryl Strawberry, Dan Quisenberry and John Mayberry Sr. Selecting Strawberry for the outfield and Mayberry Sr. at first base (thereby disqualifying Mayberry Jr.) would leave only Quintin Berry, Ken Berry and Faye Thronberry available for the other two outfield spots. Continuing down this path would necessitate completing the infield and pitching staff without any other Berry. Since that did not seem possible, it became clear that a Berry would be needed for the infield, and for that to happen, I had to find another player (not named Berry) who had played some games in the outfield. Fortunately, I had options.

The full list of candidates for this team includes:

Last	First	Given
Throneberry	Marv	Marvin Eugene
Mayberry	**John**	**John Claiborn**
Goldsberry	Gordon	Gordon Frederick
Stansberry	Craig	Craig Leo
Berry	Joe	Joseph Howard
Berry	Charlie	Charles Joseph
Barberie	**Bret**	**Bret Edward**
Berry	**Sean**	**Sean Robert**
O'Berry	Mike	Preston Michael
DeBerry	**Hank**	**John Herman**
Berryhill	Damon	Damon Scott
Berry	Joe	Joseph Howard
Berry	Claude	Claude Elzy
Berry	Charlie	Charles Francis

Last	First	Given
Berry	Ken	Allen Kent
Mayberry	John	John Claiborn
Berry	Quintin	Quintin Lonell
Throneberry	**Faye**	**Maynard Faye**
Scarbery	Randy	Randy James
McGilberry	Randy	Randall Kent
Marksberry	Matt	Matthew Gates
Marberry	Firpo	Frederick
Huckleberry	Earl	Earl Eugene
Hockenbery	Chuck	Charles Marion
DeBerry	Joe	Joseph Gaddy
Strawberry	**Darryl**	**Darryl Eugene**
Berry	Tom	Thomas Haney
Quisenberry	**Dan**	**Daniel Raymond**
Berry	Joe	Jonas Arthur
Berry	**Neil**	**Cornelius John**

The Final Team

The Pitching Staff

Starting Pitcher 1 – Firpo Marberry. Firpo is the easiest choice, as he is the all-time leading berry-named winner, with a career record of 148-88 and a 3.64 ERA.

Starting Pitcher 2 – Randy Scarbery. With three career wins and 130 career innings, Randy Scarbery has the second-most wins by a "Berry."

Starting Pitcher 3 – Earl Huckleberry. Earl owns a lifetime 1-0 mark. In his one and only Major League start, Earl went 6.2 innings, allowing seven earned runs.

Starting Pitcher 4 – Chuck Hockenbery. Chuck is the one remaining berry pitcher to have started a game, so he got the nod as the number 4 starter. Chuck was 0-5 with a 5.27 ERA.

Starting Pitcher 5 – Randy McGilberry. Although never having started a game in his career, Randy got the nod over another reliever, Matt Marsberry. Randy sports a career record of 0-2 with a 4.41 ERA.

Closer – Dan Quisenberry. "The Quiz" posted a 56-46 record with a 2.76 ERA. His 244 career saves rank him 36th in MLB history.

The Outfield

Center Field – Darryl Strawberry. Although primarily a right fielder, Darryl's 221 career stolen bases suggest he has enough range to cover center field for the Berry Team.

Right Field – Faye Thronberry. This berry sported a career .236 average and .307 on-base percentage. He made the team over Ken Berry simply to fulfill the requirement not to use the same name twice.

Left Field – Gordon Goldsberry. While primarily a first baseman, Goldsberry played some outfield, which allowed the Berry Team to have a unique name at every position.

The Infield

Catcher – Hank DeBerry. Hank beat out Damon Berryhill and Charlie Berry. It pays not to be named Berry. Hank finished with a .267 batting average and .323 on-base percentage.

First Base – John Mayberry Sr. A two-time All-Star, Mayberry Sr. has the distinction of being the second-best berry-named player of all-time. His career total of 255 home runs is surpassed only by Darryl Strawberry, and he finished his career with a .263 batting average and the highest on-base percentage for a Berry with at least 1,000 at bats (.360).

Second Base – Craig Stansberry. This berry player made the team based on the uniqueness of his name. He finished his career with a .333 batting average and a .407 on-base percentage but in just 24 at-bats.

Shortstop – Bret Barberie. While primarily a second baseman, Bret did play some shortstop and third base. He finished his career with a .271 batting average, a .356 on-base percentage and 388 hits.

Third Base – Sean Berry. My final Berry Team selection was the one "pure" Berry chosen. In 2,413 Big League at-bats, Berry had 657 hits and 81 home runs (the most by someone named Berry). He also finished with a .272 batting average and a .334 on-base percentage.

Chapter Eighteen
What's in a Name? The Best and Worst Baseball Names

Overview

Some players seemed destined to play baseball, based solely on their names. How could anyone doubt the abilities of a hitter named Homer, a fielder named Fielder or a pitcher named Armstrong? Of course, the same name might have different meanings, depending on a player's position. For example, Homer, while a great name for a hitter, is not such a great name for a pitcher. Similarly, because the letter "K" denotes a strikeout in baseball, the name Kay or Kaye seems much more appropriate for a pitcher than for a hitter.

The best and worst names teams are a list, by position, of some of the best and worst descriptive names for a baseball player.

Fun Facts
- While some ballplayers have the nickname Homer or Homerun, only 12 players have had the actual given name Homer (first name only). Interestingly, two catchers – Dixie Howell and Howie Howworth –did not use their given name of Homer (probably due to their lack of power – 12 and zero career home runs, respectively).
- Having the name Homer has not proved to be an omen. Of the 12 players with the name Homer, the most career home runs hit was 18 by outfielder Homer Summa.

- One pitcher actually goes by the name Homer (Bailey), despite his actual given name being David DeWitt. How's that for confidence?
- While nobody has sported the last name "Error," Walt Dropo sure is a close match. The first baseman was certainly not true to his name, however, posting a lifetime .992 fielding percentage. Not to be outdone, there also were a couple of klutzes (Clyde Kluttz and Mickey Klutts).
- Over 40 players have had the name Walker, but only one player has ever had the last name Walk. Ironically, he was a pitcher.
- Only two players have had the last name Kay(e). Bill Kay was a right fielder with 60 career at-bats with no strikeouts and Justin Kaye was a pitcher with three career K's in three innings pitched.
- Only one player had the last name Wacker (Charles) and, ironically, he was a pitcher.
- One player has had the given name Ace (Ace Adams) and, as luck would have it, he was a pitcher. It is worth noting that there have been three players whose last name began with Ace (Jose and Juan Acevedo and Alfredo Aceves), although not pronounced as Ace. All three of them also were pitchers.
- Two players have had the name Hitt (Roy and Bruce). However, both were pitchers.
- Looking for some power? Eight players have had the last name Power(s). Vic Power had more career home runs than all of the other Power(s) combined.

- With 300 career wins, Early Wynn is the only Hall of Fame pitcher appropriately so named, as win he did, early and often.
- Five players in the modern era have had the last name Armstrong, four of them pitchers.
- Only one player has had the last name Best (pitcher Karl Best). That makes him the Best and only.
- There has been one player with the name Strike (John) and one with the name Striker (Jake). Both were pitchers. It's hard to dispute the big difference between a pitcher who throws strikes and one who is a striker.
- The 1880s actually featured a player with the last name Suck. Tony Suck was credited with being a catcher, shortstop and center fielder.
- There has been one player with the last name Krapp. He lasted two years. In his rookie season in 1911, he pitched 222 innings and went 13-9 with a 3.41 ERA. In 1912, he pitched his final season, going 2-5 with a 4.60 ERA – thus the origination of the phrase, "He played like Krapp."
- The Federal League (which was in existence from 1913 to 1915) saw one player by the name of John Misse. His one and only year in baseball, he batted .196, truly living up to his name (miss).
- One of the most descriptive names for a pitcher belongs to Josh Outman (given his job to record outs, of course).
- Baseball has had 10 Wise players (Archie, Hugh, Casey, DeWayne, Matt, Nick, Rick, Roy, Sam, Bill) but only one Smart player (pitcher J.D. Smart).
- One current Major League pitcher has the distinction of being Godley (Zach).

The Best and Worst

Pos.	Best	Worst
P	Ace Adams	Bob Walk or Taijuan Walker (numerous other Walkers)
P	Josh Outman	Erik Plunk
P	Early Winn (Win)	Bruce or Roy Hitt
P	Justin Kaye	Gene Krapp
P	Jack Armstrong	Grant Balfour (ball four)
P	Charles Silver King	Kevin Slowey
P	Jack Fanning	Sean Doolittle
P	John Strike	Evan Meek or Roy Meeker
P	Bill Dammann (Da Man)	Brian Allard (all lard)
P	Frank or Tom Funk	J.J. Putz
P	Jeff or Ron Musselman (Muscle Man)	Hank Grampp (gramp)
P	Jimmy Key	Brent Gaff (Gaffe)
P	Urban Shocker	Pete Loos (lose)
P	Chief Bender	Aaron Small or Walt Smallwood
P	Karl Best	Joe Stanka
P	Rick Wise or JD Smart	Eric Ames (Aims)
P	Zach Godley	
P	Don Grate (Great), Mark Grater (Greater)	
P	Russ Heman (He Man)	
P	Eddie Quick	
P	Pete Rambo	

Pos.	Best	Worst
P	Dick/Ray Starr (Star)	
P	Bill Swift	
P	Jim/Mike/Roy Golden	
OF	Fielder Jones, Homer Summa, John/Bruce Fileds, Larry Walker, Ken Singleton, Carroll Hardy, Bill Goodenough, Jamal Strong, Sy Studley, Buck Thrasher, Randy Winn	Bill Kay, Jack Little, Charlie/Jim Small
1B	Prince/Cecil Fielder, Jim Steels, Vic Power, Al Flair	Walt Dropo
2B	Homer Bush, Ray Morehart (More heart), Charlie Starr (Star)	Joe Panik (Panic)
3B	Don Money	Mickey Klutts, Fred Eunick (eunuch)
SS	Tommy Field, Pat Rockett (Rocket), Hal Quick	Boob Fowler (Fouler), Tony Suck, Roy Smalley
C	George Armstrong, Farmer Steelman, Earl Battey (Batty), Lew Drill, Bill Starr (Star), Bob Swift	Klyde Kluttz, William Outen,

Chapter Nineteen
A Look Ahead to Volume II

Some of the potential themes for the next book include:

Object Team: Take a seat on a (Johnny) Bench that sits outside my (T.J.) House. If it gets too cold, come inside. I do not (Don) Lock my (Bert) Dorr. This team will consist of players with objects as part of their surname.

Alcohol Team: At the risk of being called a (Billy) Lush, please have a (Ed) Stein filled with (Ed) Pabst. If beer is not your beverage of choice, perhaps a (Ray) Flask(amper) of (Gene) Rye or (Nick) Rum(below) will be more to your liking. This team will be comprised of things you might find in a bar.

Musical Team: How about a (Vogel)song by Hendrix or (Vern) Rap(p) by Rhymes. I don't mean to toot my (Sam) Horn or beat my own (Lan)drum but I play a mean (Steve) Sax and a great (Frank) Viola. This theme team is formed by players that have a music/musician name.

Legal Team: If you ever get caught breaking the (Vern) Law as part of an (Al) Heist, I will take your (George) Case so you don't wind up in (Rafael) (Betan)court. If you should go to trial, I'll be sure that you get your (David) Justice. This team contains legal terms and things associated with the law or law enforcement.

<u>Son Team:</u> Players with surnames that begin or end with Son.

<u>Ski Team:</u> Players with surnames that end with Ski.

<u>Religion/Biblical Team:</u> Whether you go to (Ryan) Church or (Johnny) Temple, are (Hosea) Siner or an Angel (Pagan), believe in (Felix) Moses or place your (Tony) (De) Fate with the (Dave) Pope. If you have a biblical or religious name you may appear on this team.

<u>Military Team:</u> Admiral (Brad) Halsey and General Douglass (Mac) MacArthur are two that you want with you if you ever go to (Jack) War(hop). Don't bring any (Nate) Spears to battle as you will want to have your (Joe) Guns(on) a blazing if you plan on putting a (Al) Halt to your enemies (Harry) Spies. This team will have military leaders, weapons or other battle terms.

<u>Water Team:</u> I have a (Harlin) Pool and a (Simon) Pond. I think a Pond is best for you. (Ben) Wade into the (Fred) Waters down by the (Ernie) Shore but be careful not to jump into the (Gary) (Timber)lake and avoid the rushing (Mickey) Rivers. If your name is associated with water/wetness you may be on this team.

Do you have a theme you would like me to explore? If so, send me an email at Paul@alltimethemedteam.com or tweet me at @themed_teams. Thanks again for reading!

About the author

Paul Steinman is a computer consultant and avid sports fan. He grew up in New Hyde Park and Great Neck, New York where he competed in a variety of sports developing a keen interest in baseball and its rich history.

Paul graduated from the University of Pennsylvania with a BA in computer mathematics. While in college, Paul earned 4 varsity letters in wrestling, served as an officer of the Alpha Tau Omega Fraternity and continued his interest in baseball by developing a computer program that compared baseball statistics of retired players against current players in an effort to predict future performance.

Writing has always been a passion and he has published several articles in trade journals on a variety of topics including, benchmarking, the impact of the introduction of the Euro on information systems, the art of a successful contractor's bid and use of management metrics in running a business. Authoring a book has been an elusive goal of his until the release of "The All-Time Themed Baseball Teams, Volume 1."

Other than writing, Paul enjoys spending time with his family, coaching youth teams, skiing and has competed in and holds various power lifting records.

You can follow him on twitter @themed_teams.